THE SOFT-HACKLED FLY
and
TINY SOFT HACKLES

A Trout Fisherman's Guide

SECOND EDITION

Sylvester Nemes

STACKPOLE
BOOKS

Copyright © 1975, 2006 by Sylvester Nemes

Second edition published in 2006 by
STACKPOLE BOOKS
5067 Ritter Road
Mechanicsburg, PA 17055
www.stackpolebooks.com

All rights reserved, including the right to reproduce this book or portions thereof in any form or by any means, electronic or mechanical, including photocopying, recording, or by any information storage and retrieval system, without permission in writing from the publisher. All inquiries should be addressed to Stackpole Books, 5067 Ritter Road, Mechanicsburg, Pennsylvania 17055.

Printed in the United States of America

10 9 8 7 6 5 4 3 2 1

Photos by the author

Library of Congress Cataloging-in-Publication Data
Nemes, Sylvester.
The soft-hackled fly and tiny soft hackles : a trout fisherman's guide / Sylvester Nemes.—2nd ed.
  p. cm.
Rev. ed. of: The soft-hackled fly / Sylvester Nemes. c1975.
ISBN-13: 978-0-8117-0151-8
ISBN-10: 0-8117-0151-4
1. Fly fishing. 2. Fly tying. 3. Hackles (Fly tying) I. Nemes, Sylvester. Soft-hackled fly. II. Title.

SH456.N45 2006
799.17'57—dc22

2006044252

Contents

Foreword 5
Preface 9

PART ONE
   Chapter I 11
   Chapter II 25
   Chapter III 31
   Chapter IV 35
   Chapter V 41
   Chapter VI 49
   Chapter VII 73
   Chapter VIII 91
   Chapter IX 103
   Chapter X 109
   Chapter XI 117
   Chapter XII 123

PART TWO
   Chapter XIII 131
   Chapter XIV 145
   Chapter XV 149
   Chapter XVI 153
   Chapter XVII 165
   Chapter XVIII 177
   Chapter XIX 179
   Chapter XX 183
   Chapter XXI 187
   Chapter XXII 199
   Chapter XXIII 205

Bibliography 213
Index 215

Anyone who has fished for a generation or more ought to have something to say however inefficient he may be. He will have had much experience; and this is necessary if you are to describe so varied a pursuit as angling, where the possibilities are so many that some incidents only repeat themselves once or twice in a lifetime. The factors which go to make up success or failure are so numerous that until you have been through the same incident often you usually misjudge it. You do not assign the right cause. You are continually making wonderful discoveries which you think will revolutionise the pursuit and prevent you from ever coming home empty.

—*Summer on the Test,*
J. W. HILLS, 1924

Foreword

Some of our best friends are dry flies and nymphs, and we do hope that the arrival of *The Soft-Hackled Fly* on the angling scene will not cause these worthies to fall into total disuse. They certainly have their place, which is in the mouths of trout, and this is the exact spot in which Sylvester Nemes has regularly positioned his "amazing new discovery"—the soft-hackled fly.

We are being facetious, of course. From the time of that famed—and possibly fabled—fishing nun, Dame Juliana Berners, the wet fly was *the* fly—the *only* artificial fly. It wasn't until the mid-19th century that anglers in England began to float their flies, first by accident, then by intent, and finally by specific design. It soon became a cult, then a philosophy of life, and eventually a religion, and F.M. Halford was its prophet.

Then came the siren call of the nymphs, the Loreleis

which lured unwary anglers from the comfort and intimacy of the stream surface and into the depths. For nearly half a century G.E.M. Skues and his fellow nymphers were barred from the chalkstreams of southern England, heretics after the manner of the early Christians; and it is perhaps ironic that the symbol of those persecuted zealots took the form of a fish! Even today, nymphs are frowned upon in England on many waters—and even here, in the land of the free.

During this adventurous period, the wet fly never fell into disuse—only into disrepute. It was a "good way to start a youngster," or a desperation measure when all else failed. But, it is our feeling, and obviously that of Syl Nemes, that it has not been the fault of technique alone that has led to the current nadir of the wet fly in America. Just as the pressing social need for basketball centers has delivered a generation of young giants to center court, so has the quest for the Holy Grail of stiff hackles filled the roosts and the fly-tying benches with the distillation of 50 years of in-bred fighting gamecocks. The sophisticated angler would not leave a fly shop satisfied until his lips were literally punctured by the ultimate stiff-hackle test.

It became difficult to tell a wet fly from a dry, except for the position of the wings. Actually, as Syl points out in this book, the proper wet hackle can be as difficult to procure as stiff, surface-riding dry-fly hackle—but it is available. We commend his patterns, his philosophy and his techniques to you.

We have fished with Syl Nemes in Michigan and in Colorado, and we have seen him deliver fish when other anglers of quality were flushed with defeat.

We have also benefited from the good works of this

streamside Samaritan who lurks behind trees and steps out at the propitious moment to offer his *aqua regia* to the deflated angler. On our second trip together, while on the Frying Pan near Aspen, he crossed my palm with three soft-hackles which I accepted with a smile and deposited in my fly box.

It wasn't until a year later that I was driven to their use —and I still can't be certain that the fantastic results I had with the   were not due primarily to my consummate skill as an angler! But, in truth, I feel in retrospect that it was the fly and not the fly fisher who triumphed that memorable afternoon. (A fresh shipment of one dozen soft-hackles has recently arrived from Nemes' bench, and I shall once more test them against the declining desk-dulled reflexes of a flabby fly fishermen who needs all the help he can get.)

I will fish these soft-hackles with love, with confidence and with little else. I will drift them with the current, letting the hackles reflect the action of the tiny mini-currents of the stream, and with no jerks. A jerk at *one* end of the line is enough.

Without making any forecasts—for I am at heart a coward and content to record the past—I will be interested to see what happens when the hard facts of soft hackles reach more and more anglers. Nor shall I go so far as to suggest that any name such as "Sylvester Nemes" could ever become a household word—unless it be used by an irate wife in condemnation of an absent angler.

The soft-hackled fly offers the versatility, the utility and little of the futility of other flies in general day-to-day application. It offers the novice a definite leg-up, and as much challenge to the experienced angler as his expertise can summon. For the skillful use of the wet fly has long been considered by older and wiser heads to be the most artful of all angling techniques; the soft-hackle fly merely brings the wet fly out of the mists of history and into the mainstream of the difficult and challenging waters we fish today.

DON ZAHNER
Dorset, Vermont
July 21, 1975

Preface

The term, soft-hackled fly, is used generically throughout this book, and applies to a class of wingless, subaqueous flies, the hackles of which come mostly from birds such as partridge, woodcock, grouse, snipe, and starling.

No dry fly fisherman has challenged me to write it. It has been undertaken because the soft-hackled fly and the mending method of fishing it, outlined in the book, are rarely, if ever, discussed in angling literature published in America.

The author has never seen the soft-hackled fly used by any other fisherman. My observations have been made on many of the finest and most famous trout waters of the country. And although mending is now popular with some steelhead fishermen in the west, it is not generally employed by trout fishermen using the sunk fly.

The soft-hackled fly is not to be easily found in even the best stocked fly shops in the country. Yet, the flies are elementary and quick to tie from easily obtainable materials. And the mending method of fishing the fly is so simple that a beginner can learn it immediately...and a dry fly purist, depending on how dry he is, a little longer.

The book is also written for many of the older, dry fly fishermen I have met who embraced the sport late in life. In three-day fishing schools in Vermont, Colorado, or Montana, these men have learned to fish dry, but have lost a great deal of fishing fun by not learning to fish a sunk fly downstream.

Because the soft-hackled fly is nymph-like, the book may help to show practiced and would-be nymph fishermen a new way to fish their favorite nymph patterns, or to try the soft-hackled flies instead. The instructions here eliminate the need for the average fly fisherman to be an entomologist. He need not know the difference between a stonefly nymph and a small mayfly nymph. He can forget emergence dates, fly sex, and maturity or immaturity. He can travel from one stream to another, east or west, and enjoy the sport as it was meant to be enjoyed in the beginning...without cult, ritual, and mystery.

Because history is important and of interest to many fly fishermen, the book also traces the evolution of the soft-hackled fly in angling literature. The repeated discoveries of its mention in the most highly regarded books on fly fishing is quite remarkable. Even in the very first English writings about fly fishing, a soft-hackled fly, the Donne fly, is the first of twelve in the list prepared by Dame Juliana Berners, in 1496.

With so noble a beginning, it is the purpose of this book to restore the soft-hackled fly to its rightful place.

May, 1975   S.N.

PART ONE

Chapter I

I saw my first soft-hackled flies some fifteen years ago in Paul H. Young's tackle shop in Detroit, Michigan. The flies were simple, yet extremely attractive. Drab, yet enticing. The slender bodies were of silk floss in any of three colors: orange, yellow, and olive green. At the head of each fly was a partridge hackle, wound very sparsely around the hook. Lying there together, mixed in the box, the flies looked alive and natural and very much like real insects, due mostly to the minute, freckled markings on every barbule of the hackles.

Young called the flies, "P.H.Y. Partridge Spiders." His catalog advertised the flies saying, "Fished like a nymph. This is one of the best all around wet flies I ever used. Fish down and across stream, and take trout. Hackles lay back along the hook when wet, and crawl or work in the current."

That advertising message, written by one of the great bamboo rod makers of America seemed too simple, too pat. Yet the flies excited me and appealed to some facet of my fishing makeup, and I went out of the store with six of them; two orange, two yellow, and two green.

I didn't know then that these simple, two-part flies would, in a short time, shape my whole fishing future and become the nucleus of a sunk fly fishing method that would exclude every other kind of fly. It is the object of this book to show how, and perhaps why, this happened.

To retrace one's fishing steps back from the present time and the present state of the art, can be at once pleasant and enlightening, difficult and even embarrassing. One is affected first by a locale and its easily available water, and by the successes or failures recorded on this water either by the fisherman himself, or by those he happens to meet at the water's edge. The fickle fisherman will discard a certain lure, bait, or fly pattern or fishing style as soon as he finds something else more successful, or more appealing to some inner instinct.

Once addicted to fly fishing, he moves laterally or horizontally from wet-only to dry-only. From nymph most of the time, to dry some of the time; or from big, shiny streamer-only, to nymph-only; or from day fishing to night fishing. In most movements, he seeks to catch more fish or bigger fish, but finally he seeks a personal satisfaction doing what, to him, elevates him with the pleasure he's looking for. This is why the fisherman always wears the same old hat, or torn vest. Why he prefers his bamboo rod to a glass one. Why he'd rather cast a silk line instead of a plastic one. Why he sticks with a single fly or one kind of fly or one certain method instead of some other. Or even why he prefers to fish, in solitude, on an obviously less fruitful stretch of water on his favorite river, instead of jamming up with the other fishermen in the popular pool or run just around the bend.

So it was with my own fishing evolution. It started on the west side of Cleveland, in the late 30's, at least 150 miles from the nearest trout stream. True, I had Lake Erie a few blocks from home, and I can remember, first, fishing with a hand line and trolley for perch and pike as they swarmed the breakwalls and piers in search of food. Huge schools of white bass also scourged the shallows chasing madly after anything that moved. They came right in to the beaches, boiling the surface. The school moved across the water in one large mass and it was easy to catch a bushel basket full of them with a bait casting rod and multiple winding reel. This was more fun than still-fishing for perch or pike. The favorite lure for the white bass was a piece of white cloth, a quarter of an inch wide and about an inch long. The piece of cloth was stuck on to a small hook and two, three, or even four of these were tied onto a four or five foot piece of gut. The gut was attached to a small section of broom handle with screw eyes on either end, one for the casting line and the other for the gut.

The broom handle was the plug and supplied the weight one needed for the cast and it kept the "flies" up on the surface during the retrieve. The fisherman threw the plug right into the middle of the school and worked it back in jumps and jerks. The white bass went mad for it, chasing the pieces of white cloth, hooking themselves, fighting to get off, and often unhooking themselves, so that another could grab it before it was finally retrieved. Three fish, up to 10 inches long, were frequently caught at one time. And you could see it all.

Not all of the white bass fishermen used the pieces of cloth. Some used a real fly, a small white or yellow streamer type made from plain chicken feathers. I don't think they were any more effective than the cloth, but once I saw them I knew I had to try them.

The flies were available from a barber, Glen Buckel, who had a shop on Detroit Avenue, just west of the neighborhood in which I lived. I rode over there on my bike the first chance I got.

The shop was small with a window on each side of the door. One window had a display consisting of packages of hackles, tinsels, hooks, furs, chenille, paired wing quills and other fly tying materials. The other window contained a large framed card on which were attached all the materials required for a dry Quill Gordon. The finished Gordon was also stuck to the card, and I wondered how a feather, piece of quill, and slips of yellow wood duck could be turned into such a beautiful work of art.

Inside, framed colored prints of trout and salmon, hung on one of the walls. Black and white photos showed a smiling Glen with his friends standing beside, or fishing in a variety of streams. In the shop, two barber chairs were on the left, from which customers could look to the other wall on which hung long, glass cases filled with trout flies, bass flies, and even fully dressed salmon flies.

Glen Buckel had no customers when I arrived and was bent over a vise on a table in the back of the room. Here were cabinets and closets which contained more stocks of fly tying materials. Rod cases and sections of bamboo rods in various stages of completion leaned in a corner of the room. As I found out later, Glen made his bamboo rods from raw cane.

At that point, at the age of sixteen or seventeen, I now know that I had my initial major romantic experience. It was love at first sight. What I was in love with is hard to say for I had never before seen a trout fly, a trout, or a trout stream nor had I ever read a single word about fishing for them.

Glen didn't pay much attention to me and went right on tying the flies. Feeling like an intruder, I inched closer to him. He was waiting for me to speak first. I don't know why, but I felt embarrassed. I started asking silly, elementary questions about fly tying and fly fishing. Like many a professional's attitude towards the rank beginner, Glen was so bored, he couldn't answer. I got nothing out of him except the suggestion that I visit the main branch of the public library in downtown Cleveland where I could find all the information I wanted on fly tying and fly fishing.

Before I left the shop, however, I bought fifteen or twenty cents worth of hooks and white and yellow chicken feathers for the white bass flies, and started a hobby that has been a real and important part of my life for more than thirty years.

My first tyings were terrible. I had no vise, no hackle pliers, no thread bobbin. I fashioned a vise from a pair of square nosed pliers, put the hook in the jaws and wrapped a stout rubber band around the handles. I made a pair of hackle pliers from a piece of coat hanger, and from the same material, I invented my own thread bobbin, which I still use today. My mother supplied thread and flosses from her crocheting and sewing basket.

I couldn't figure out how to get the hackle fibres to

stand out perpendicular to the hook shank as they did on Glen's flies. I thought each fibre was tied in separately. I couldn't tie a half-hitch. The tinsel wouldn't lie flat. It was frustrating and I was getting nowhere.

There was nothing left to do but take Glen's advice and head for the library. Over the period of a year, I read every book on fly tying and fly fishing the library had to offer. I would take home, for seven days at a time, books by Halford, Skues, LaBranche, Hewitt, Hills, Bergman, Knight, and many others. In one of the British books, I saw photographs of the Test River and of the village of Stockbridge on that river and the Grosvener Hotel, where fly fishermen met to try this great stream. How easy it was for me to read these books. What fascination they held for me! How inexplicable that a teenage kid from the west side of Cleveland, without a single fly fishing friend or relative, would spend his days and nights reading about a subject so foreign and trying to tie flies for trout in streams as yet unseen and unfished.

Armed with the knowledge I was getting from all the books, I visited Glen more and more. He warmed gradually for it was obvious I was as enthusiastic a pupil as he had ever encountered. I would show him the flies I tied and he would show me where and how I made mistakes. He taught me the right way to set and tie wings, to make half-hitches, to wind hackles around the shank, and to handle tinsels. He talked with me like a streamside brother. He told me of the great trout streams in northern Michigan where he had originally come from and where he spent two weeks every year on vacation. He spoke of trout streams near Kane, Pennsylvania which were, he said, the closest to Cleveland.

The more he talked, the more I knew that soon I would have to fish one of these rivers, to be baptised or, better yet, to be married forever. The courtship had gone on long enough.

So, in the spring of 1938, I made plans to fish the streams near Kane. I had been working at odd jobs around the neighborhood, cleaning a bakery, selling newspapers or whatever I could get. I had the money to buy a pair of boots, a fly rod and reel, with enough left over for the Greyhound bus ride to Kane and back, and room and board for the weekend. And I had my own flies.

My mother worried about the trip. To her it was an odyssey to the ends of the earth. I was going alone and I didn't know a soul in Kane. How would I get to the rivers from town? Where would I stay and what would I eat? I told her I could take care of myself, and that I could hitchhike to the streams or walk if I had to.

The bus left Cleveland late in the evening. I never slept a wink, and by dawn I could see the purple-black outlines of the low mountains in north central Pennsylvania. All that I had read and dreamed about was going to come true. Or was it? As it turned out, I couldn't cast and I couldn't make the fly float. I couldn't wade among the slippery rocks, and went down in the icy spring water more than once. In the British books that I had read earlier, I had seen the patterns of the Butcher and the Alexandra, known in England as killer flies and outlawed on many streams there. I had copied them for the Kane trip where I tried them again and again. Nothing came to them then, and I haven't used them since.

I can't remember if I caught a single fish during that weekend, but I did see some small trout in the basket of another fisherman and their beauty of form and color, not to mention the mountains, the clear water and pure air, convinced me that the baptism was worth it.

Later, back in Cleveland, I was fishing Rocky River with ringed-eyed flies and spinners, but now, at least, I was stuck to a fly rod. The river divides Cleveland from Lakewood and runs through Metropolitan Park. I don't know the condition of the river at the present time, but back then it was quite clear and delightful, with some rapids and some slow pools and many sharp bends against small cliffs of shale. As the river's name implies, there were many rocks which split the current and also hid some very nice black bass.

A fast retrieve was necessary to keep the spinner blade turning in the slower water, and I learned the "figure 8" left hand retrieve. After a while, I was able to read the water, and would move from one pool to another looking for places that resembled the source of the previous strike.

In addition to artificial lures, I was also using live helgrammites with the fly rod during these ventures. Since the river was full of them, they could be easily caught in a piece of netting by upsetting rocks in the faster current. Once captured, the helgrammite was secured to the hook with a small rubber band slipped over its abdomen. These larval forms of the dobson fly were mean and evil looking with powerful pinchers at their heads, which would grab onto a finger or equally well onto the lip of the bass which went for the bait.

The fly-and-spinner combinations on a fly rod followed me into the army in 1942, and I used them with great success for rainbow on the San Gabriel River, near Los Angeles where I was stationed for a time. In that same river, I was fishing a wooly worm, which was then becoming popular on the west coast. The ringed-eyed fly-and-spinner combination has almost disappeared from American trout fishing, due perhaps to considerable "fly fishing only" legislation. In the early forties, however, it was a very popular way to fish. One could buy the flies separately and attach them to his own spinners, or buy complete fly-spinner rigs. These flies were very colorful and almost always contained some red. Today, most fly material catalogs do not even list ringed-eyed hooks.

In December of 1943, the Army gave me, and our fighter control squadron, passage on a crowded troop ship to England. Our destination turned out to be a small village right on the banks of the Hampshire Avon. I did not fish that river for trout as the season was still closed, but one day in February I ghillied for a titled gentleman who owned salmon fishing rights and helped him land a 20 lb specimen he had hooked on spinning gear.

In April, our squadron moved to an airfield at Andover, just seven or eight miles from Stockbridge, and the Test River. What a coincidence! What a stroke of fate! As soon as it was possible, I was on a bus to the village and that fabled stretch of water.

The Grosvener Hotel was there, matching the photographs I had seen earlier in the British angling books in Cleveland. The Test, not far from the hotel, ran smoothly and evenly, with long weeds limpid as hair, obscuring the white lime bottom. The river seemed to move as if it were one large mass of glass, with a nearly uniform depth from one bank to the other. Closeup, one could see right through it, but a few steps back, the smooth, even surface became a mirror that reflected the sky and the trees and hid all that was beneath.

Looking into the river, I felt the temptation to fish as I had never felt it before and hurried back to the hotel. I found out, however, that the entire river was a private preserve from beginning to estuary, though I heard that the Leckford Club might permit a GI to fish on its four miles of water upstream. It was true! That same day I met the club secretary who informed me that wartime conditions prevented the club members from getting to the river in any number and that American soldiers were invited to fish in their absence. What a nice bit of reverse "Lend Lease." With permission granted, the visitor had to abide by club rules: dry fly only upstream to rising trout or grayling; beat-fishing on the number assigned for the day or evening; fishing from the bank only, with no wading; and killing of all fish caught.

The secretary told me that I could come whenever I wanted and to simply report in to Mr. Bains, the river keeper, at his small cottage near the middle beat.

I had brought no equipment from America, and so purchased an eight foot, two-piece rod from a tackle shop in Andover where I had no choice in selection since it was the only rod in the store. The joints were of the Hardy spiral lockfast type and the windings were close-spaced the whole length of the rod in typical British fashion. The action was medium, much like American rods.

Mr. Bains was an older man, taciturn, yet friendly. He offered me one of the club rods complete with a Hardy reel and double tapered silk line, but the rod felt top heavy to me since it was about ten feet long. I was anxious to try my own new rod in any case, so I was lent only a reel and line and knotted silk worm leader. I had my own drys from Glen, which Mr. Bains thought were well tied, but too large for the river. He gave me a small tin box with several Test patterns in it: olives, iron blues, orange and ginger quills, and the Welshman's buttons, in 12's, 14's and 16's.

The Leckford water of the Test was about four miles long and was divided into ten beats, the same number as the membership of the club. Members at that time included a Vice Admiral of the British fleet air arm, the owner of a well-known chain of department stores, a doctor, a lawyer, and six other well-endowed gentlemen.

Beat numbers were marked on stakes driven into the bank on both sides of the river. Crossing the river meant walking back to one of the bridges. There was no wading allowed and one fished dry shod. Bains took me to my beat and explained that I was not to fish until I saw a trout rise.

Riverbank foliage was trimmed impeccably; even the weeds were kept low. Tree branches that might interfere with false casting were not present. Benches were placed along every beat so the fisherman could sit to watch the water for the rising fish. No wonder the English call this, "the contemplative sport."

I sat and waited, my eyes glued to the river. After a short time, I began to see swallows buzzing the surface of the river, dipping down here and there for the first flies of the hatch. Then the rises started on the river, slowly at first, then faster, until I could see a half dozen fish feeding immediately above and below me. I tried the closest fish. He rose and I struck, but too fast. Another try on another fish and I lipped the fish, losing the fly. After quite a few more tries, I finally got one, a fish of about a pound and a half. I was starting to throw more slack, to give the fly a longer, natural float before any drag occurred. It seemed better to wait a second to set the hook after I saw the rise, than to strike immediately. I fished out my whole beat and raised many fish, but I caught only one other, slightly larger than the first.

These two fish, on my first day on the Test, were the largest I had caught in about seven years of fly fishing. Reading now, about how difficult it is to catch Test trout, because of their "education," selectivity and aversion to drag, not to mention the nature of the clear slow water with its tricky currents, I think I did quite well.

I continued to fish the Test through May and the first part of June, and again during July of 1945. I learned to strike slowly, to stalk the fish from a low position on one knee, and to throw slack. I caught many "brace" of brown trout and a few grayling, a fish the Test fly fisher disdains and calls "gray bob." The largest fish I saw taken was caught by a gentleman on a different beat from mine. I helped net the prize after it fought for some 25 minutes on a size 16 Orange Quill. The big trout weighed one ounce less than five pounds.

How the British fish the Test and other chalkstreams is a good example of how fishermen are apt to have their own way of things. Most American anglers would not agree with the system. There have also been some British anglers and writers who thought the dry-fly-only rules were all wet and proved it. Now I understand these rules have been modified, and some clubs have succumbed to limited sunk fly fishing upstream.

As I write these pages, I reflect once more on the generosity of the members of the Leckford Club. I don't think my youth allowed me to fully appreciate the privilege of fishing a river as special as the Test. Mr. Bains has departed as, I suspect sadly, have many of the fine gentlemen I met there during those troubled years. Perhaps it's always sad to reflect on the good fishing and good fishing friends of days gone by.

Chapter II

After the war, I pursued a college education in my home state of Ohio. I built my first bamboo rod and was tying more and more flies. I saw Glen Buckel only rarely, but on our first reunion after I returned from Europe, he seemed anxious to question me about the fishing on the Test. He, too, had read much about the river. He knew that only a privileged few ever get to fish it and that only a few more would even be permitted to walk along its banks. At that time, few Americans had done either. Piscatorially, I had achieved a high distinction and Glen's esteem, which was obvious, made me feel important and good.

Now, however, fishing was restricted to spring and summer breaks from college when I would hitchhike from Cleveland to Grayling or to Baldwin, Michigan. I fished parts of Pennsylvania, too, and revisited Kane, where I performed better than I had during my first trip several years before.

I had returned to wet fly fishing, mostly with bucktails in the early part of the year and small, winged wet patterns later on. I always carried dry flies with me in case a hatch came on, but looking back on it, I seem to remember very few first-rate hatches during daylight hours.

What a difference between the British ways I had seen and the American to which I had returned. Here I was sharing the river with worm fishermen, egg fishermen, and other fly fishermen. They came and went in front of you, upstream and down. The coarser the tackle and style, the greater the animosity. I feel that most American fly fishermen would prefer to fish finer or only with a dry fly, but that on most all-systems rivers, there is constant competition with live bait or hardware, which seems to compel a resort to large bucktails. One rarely sees good, healthy hatches on these rivers and even when they do occur, the fish do not seem to feed on the insects.

After college, I never moved far from the midwestern centers of Detroit, Cleveland, and Chicago, and for a time was limited in my fishing to opening days and a few weekends on the Au Sable, Pere Marquette, Little Manistee, the Boardman, and other rivers in Michigan. With flies only, either bucktail or wet, I was catching my fair share of the average size fish in these rivers, but rarely would put into anything as big as twenty inches.

Yet these waters held big trout and local fly fishers caught them regularly. The secret was to fish at night with big, nondescript hair and feather flies, dry or wet. Fred Koernke, one of these local fishermen, lived in Lovells, Michigan, on the north branch of the Au Sable. He, too, had come from Cleveland, but had given up the city life in favor of regular access to a trout stream. He and his wife, Hazel, operated the Pines Restaurant, and every evening after closing, Fred was out on one of the branches of the Au Sable or some one of the smaller creeks not too far from home. He rarely fished during the day time.

The restaurant was a meeting place for many local trout buffs. In addition to meals, Fred sold flies, rods and reels surrounded by a decor featuring two six-pound nocturnal browns mounted on the wall. I would guess he caught several specimens of that size every season.

I got in the habit of fishing the north branch quite often because it had no canoe traffic on it and because it was restricted to the use of flies. I ate every meal I possibly could at the Pines Restaurant and would often drive forty miles out of my way, hoping Fred would invite me with him on one of his evening ventures. For a while, as an outsider, I felt I might have more chance of getting an invitation to the White House than to be invited to one of Fred's hotspots. But he finally did offer and I gladly accepted.

We left the restaurant about 9 P.M. and drove for about half an hour in a downstream direction. At the end of a long pole fence, he stopped and turned into a small rutted road. We parked and walked about a quarter of a mile towards the river. There was still enough daylight left to see our way over the rotted tree stumps and through tall spreading ferns. The river below was quite fast and its sound was evident before we could see it. We clambered down the steep bank and sat on a large felled tree trunk. Now, we waited. We were waiting, Fred said, to hear the first sounds of the whip-poor-will. He also kept watch in the waning light for the first signs of the "caddis" hatch.

Misnamed in Michigan, the "caddis" hatch is really the hatch of the large, burrowing mayfly. Adult insects will have a wing span of up to two inches. The nymphs of the species, called wigglers, are large enough to be impaled on a hook as live bait. No other hatch in Michigan causes so much excitement among fly fishermen. Every trout in the river will gorge himself on these nymphs, and it is during this time that fish of over five and six pounds are taken. The fly rarely comes off before dark.

The light was fading fast now, and the whip-poor-wills were answering themselves up and down the river. Then, in the last remaining light from the sky, we saw through the trees the first "caddis" flies winging their way up stream. Fred said it was time to get in. He directed me to a spot just a few feet down from the tree trunk while he went downstream some fifty yards.

Though it was pitch black from the surface of the river to the tops of the trees, I could hear the trout sucking in the "caddis" here and there. How acute my hearing had become, being robbed of sight. I started casting to the sounds, having made sure I was far enough in the river to clear the back cast. Immediately I had a strike. The sound from the rise to the artificial was louder and more vociferous than the regular suckings of the spent naturals. I landed a fish of about fourteen inches, and started in again. I was asking myself where the seven and eight inch fish were that I normally caught in water like this during the daylight hours, when I heard quite a large commotion in the vicinity of my fly and set the hook again. I had a good fish on this time, but the line went slack.

I brought the line in to check the fly and turned on my flashlight to find that the fly was gone. I shined the light onto the water and there were no more "caddis." The hatch had just gotten started and yet it was all over. I could see Fred's light moving up and down on the bank and I climbed out to join him. He didn't do much better than I did and we walked back silently dodging the stumps and brushing through the tall ferns.

The experience was a typical attempt to fish the "caddis" hatch in Michigan. The nonresident angler, limited to a weekend or a couple of days now and then, doesn't stand a chance of being there when the flies are really on. It will be a hit-or-miss proposition, much like daylight dry fly fishing. If the foreigner cannot be there every day or every evening for a period of two or three weeks, he will find only a few moments when all the conditions are ideal for his floating fly. This is why the "locals" do so well, and there is no competing with them.

I have tried night fishing on the Au Sable, the Pere Marquette and other rivers in Michigan, and I have caught fish over the twenty inch mark, though not many. On these waters, this is the only way to get big fish with the fly. But there is so much more visual enjoyment when fishing in daylight. A great deal of what I fish for seems to be gone, once the whip-poor-wills begin their night time answering service.

Chapter III

It was on the north branch of the Au Sable, that I first tried Paul Young's Partridge Spiders. I started fishing the fly the same way I fished winged wets and bucktails. In slower water I would jerk the fly in its downstream course, and in faster water I would let it drift freely. I always threw a fairly tight line so that I could feel the strike even when I couldn't see the fly or the swirl of the fish. The fly performed well from the start, but gradually I noticed an increase in the amount of action when the fly was drifting freely in any kind of water. The longer the natural drift, the better the results.

With a tight line, the fly would run down without drag for a short time, then start to cross over to my side as the line bellied in the current. I did not like that part of the cast and was trying to change it. I wanted longer, natural drifts and started throwing a slack line with "S's" in the cast, much like I did with the dry fly for the Test trout. This kept the fly "over there" longer, in the eddies or pockets or flats, which I read to be good holding water.

Instead of casting straight across, I started casting upstream a little, moving the rod tip toward my bank to keep the line tight to signal the strike, then moving the rod tip toward the other bank as the line and the fly passed my level in their downstream phase of the trip. To lengthen the amount of free drift, when the cast was spent, I would let out line, the amount governed by the current.

Of the three colors, the green, yellow, and orange, both the fish and I were partial to the orange. If I fished strange water anywhere, I always started out with this color, but would try the others if it didn't work after a half hour or so. I believe, however, that the three colors pretty well represent almost all the colors of insect life, nymph or emerging fly, one might find on any stream in the country.

I was so enamored of these partridge-hackle flies, that gradually my fly box contained nothing else, in the three colors and in sizes from 8 to 14. My own tyings of them became even more slender and sparse than the first examples I bought from Young.

I gave up all fishing of streamers or bucktails in daylight hours and rarely tied and used wet flies with any wings whatsoever on them.

My confidence in the soft-hackled fly gained each time I went out. I could follow other fly fishermen down the river who would fish a nice stretch of water without a single rise, and take fish right at their backs. When they asked what I used, I would tell them and they would act puzzled. They never heard of the fly. When I produced a couple, they would say "is that all there is to them?"

I would fish the fly at any time of day on any water, and be surprised to see it take trout even during a hatch. Normally, the arrival of a hatch means an end to wet fly or nymph fishing. Not so with these soft-hackles. Without knowing what fly was on the water, I would use the yellow-bodied fly when the natural insect was very light or yellow, the orange-bodied fly when the natural was reddish or brown, and the green-bodied one when the natural was blue or dun or any other dark shade.

With a floating line, the fly was just below the surface of the water. I could see the rise in the form of a swirl or bulge in the water, but I really didn't have to see it, because I could feel it as well. This was what I really liked about the soft-hackle system.

The classic upstream nymph fishing method requires keen eyesight with which many anglers are not endowed. One must watch for a "brown shadow," or a bulge, a tightening of the line or leader, or some other mysterious, intuitive message. But, I believe a blind man could successfully fish my flies in the manner described.

So, after twenty years of fly fishing, wet fly and dry, upstream and down, America and England, I had come back to a simple, two-part fly with only a body and game bird hackle, and a fishing system that was easy and productive, satisfying and esthetic.

During the next five years, however, it was to get even better. Here's why. I discovered other soft-hackled flies besides those made with partridge feathers. I started fishing western streams with fast, shallow riffles, even more suitable to the soft-hackled fly. I began to fish for steelhead; and I read Jock Scott's book, *Greased Line Fishing for Salmon*.

Chapter IV

In 1968, my work as a free lance industrial photographer took me to western Wyoming, Idaho, and Montana. I had never seen or fished the famous rivers in those states before: the Wind, Madison, Yellowstone, Rock Creek, Gallatin, Snake, and others. The fisherman, on first seeing these rivers is awed by their size and speed, the clarity of the water, the openness of the valleys through which the streams run and the breathtaking beauty of magnificent Rocky Mountain vistas all around.

In these rivers the water is riffly and "flat," barely skimming the earth's surface, except in canyons where fishing is almost impossible. There is much free or open water to fish, a great deal of fly-only water, and there are relatively few fishermen. In addition, the average trout will be six or seven inches longer than those in the midwest or east, and a four pound brown or rainbow barely raises an eyebrow.

I have been lucky enough, since 1968, to find both professional work and great fishing pleasure in those western states at least twice every year. On such trips, I have fished the soft-hackled fly almost exclusively, but I must admit trying out such local "western" tyings as the Bitch Creek, Montana Nymph, and the wooly worms. These are big, ugly, weighted flies, most of which represent the prevalent stonefly nymph or even the helgrammite. For me, casting them is difficult and unenjoyable. Most fishermen there cast them upstream, roll them down on the bottom like a worm and set the hook when the line stops moving in the current. This was not my preferred way of fishing the fly, so I stuck with the soft-hackles and improved the method of fishing them after I read *Greased Line Fishing for Salmon*.

In his book, first published in 1935 and just recently reissued, Jock Scott tells how A.H.E. Wood landed 3,490 salmon from 1913 to 1934 on a Scottish river using small, slimly dressed flies and a greased, floating line.

Mr. Wood's method of "mending" the line to increase the natural float or drift of the fly was exactly what I had been looking for to eliminate drag or the bellying of the line, and still permit me to fish downstream and to feel the rise without the necessity of seeing it.

With this method, the fisherman can fish the fly in a natural manner, the fly traveling very near the surface and presenting a side view of itself to the fish.

With the soft-hackled fly, the technique is a deadly one for trout.

What is mending? It is the lifting or raising of the

troublesome or dragging part of the line and flipping it upstream or down, without really moving the fly. To accomplish the upstream or downstream mend, one must use a floating line, and must learn to cast a slack line. I do this by throwing the line high, waiting until it is fully extended, then drawing back on it while it is still suspended, so that it falls to the water in loose "s" curves. The beginning fly fisherman, who hasn't yet learned how to throw a tight, straight line, can obviously learn to mend relatively quickly.

Most small rivers will require an upstream mend because there is usually more fast water between the fisherman and the fly. But on large rivers, the angler may find a slower current between him and the fly, which calls for a downstream mend. If the water is all in a "sheet," moving with the same velocity from bank to bank, the mending technique is not necessary at all.

As the line continues downstream, the angler must keep on mending as long as drag occurs, until the cast is fished out. To help in the process, lead the line with the rod in its downstream journey and hold it high and parallel to the surface of the water so that the mend will be easy to perform.

With the soft-hackled fly and the mending method, hooking the fish is almost automatic. First, the rise, or swirl, or splash or bulge will occur where the fly is and the action will be relayed to the angler. It is also good practice to keep one's eyes moving downstream on the area where the fly is believed to be. Striking the fish need not be forceful, merely a tightening of the rod is usually sufficient to set the hook.

It has always seemed to me that dry fly fishing is considered the higher art of trout fishing and the wet fly the lower, simply because there seems to be more to do about the dry fly. In dry fly fishing, there is the floating line and the natural, drag-free float. There is the finer leader, the greater stalking, the better knowledge of the insect life on the water and the exact imitation. More art and more science, hence greater pleasure? Maybe. But, the soft-hackled fly fished with a floating line and mended upstream and down, with fine terminal tackle, gives the most sophisticated dry fly fisherman plenty to do in the arts and science departments, and a lot more to feel in the fun department.

There is plenty of proof. The soft-hackled fly tempts trout a great deal more often. It tempts bigger trout. And it rouses the rapacity of the most lethargic trout causing it to charge from great distance or depth. That's why the take, when fishing these flies, is so powerful and so extremely physical.

In dry fly fishing, the trout, with no real urgency, reaches for the fly if it is straight over his head, but it is the fisherman who sets the hook into the fish, and the battle between fish and fisherman ensues. With the soft-hackled fly, the trout throws caution to the wind, because he's not afraid to move under the water and speeds to the fly with urgency, setting it himself. The contact is more violent and forceful, because it was the trout's decision and not the fisherman's.

Upstream fishing with a weighted or unweighted nymph can be compared in the same way. The fisherman watches for the slightest hesitancy of the line or leader, or for some hint in the water, and tightens the line to set the hook. There is really nothing to feel until that has been accomplished.

Chapter V

What is it about the soft-hackled fly that has led a fisherman like myself to entirely give up the use of all other sunk flies in fishing for trout? What special appeal does it have? What does it represent or imitate, if anything, at all? What makes it so universal that sometimes it works just as well during a hatch, as without one, and fishes equally well on almost any trout stream in the country?

Earlier British writers, by the score (as the reader will see in the next chapter), praised the soft-hackles. They were classified in many lists as general flies, meaning that they had no counterparts in real insect life. It was a good fly, they said, but they didn't know why.

Even G.E.M. Skues, who led the revolt against the exclusive use of the dry fly on southern British chalkstreams, apparently did not know why. In his, *The Way of a Trout with a Fly,* first published in 1921, he said:

> Fished directly upstream, a wet fly (whether winged or not), which is hackled with a stiff cock's hackle, has thrown away one of its chief advantages, the mobility of the hackle. In fact, one might be inclined to think that if a hackle were not needed to break the fall or suggest life, such a fly might best be dressed without a hackle. A hen's hackle, or a small bird's hackle, would respond to every movement of the current, and would thus suggest an appearance of life in action, which is very fascinating. The Yorkshire hackles and Stewart's famous trio of 'spiders', so called, are based on this theory. What these flies really represent cannot always be certainly predicated. Doubtless the hackles in some cases suggest the wings and legs of hatched-out insects, drowning or drowned and tumbled by the current, and in others they suggest some nondescript, struggling subaqueous creature. In either case the mobility suggests life.

"Life" of what order or class of insects . . . ephemera (mayfly) or trichoptera (caddis)?

My answer to this question, when beginning the work for this book in 1972, was the ephemera.

I was convinced the soft-hackled fly suggested any of the four types of nymphs, or their duns, of the mayfly family . . . the order of insects generally considered to be of the most interest to fly fishermen. In this order there are: 1) flat or clinging nymphs such as the March Brown; 2) swimming nymphs such as the Pale Evening Dun; 3) crawling nymphs such as the Blue-winged Olive; 4) and burrowing nymphs such as the Michigan mayfly wiggler.

The various nymphs prefer different kinds of streambottoms from mud to sand to stone to large flat rocks, and bottoms with weeds and without. The shapes of the nymphs differ considerably; some long and slender, some short and fat, and some wide and flattened. Some rivers can actually produce all four kinds in a very few feet, and it has been observed by many fishing writers that two and three or more different kinds of nymphs can be hatching from the same water simultaneously.

This hatching occurs, entomologists say, when the nymph swallows water or air or both to expand its muscles and split the outer skin along the top of the thorax. This can happen on the surface or underneath, in which case the new dun elevates to the surface in some sort of gas balloon which keeps him dry. At this point, we have an unwet or dry dun actually submerged! I believed this was the reason why the sunk soft-hackled fly was taken so well during a hatch.

All of the above, as I said, was written during the latter months of 1972. Since that time, however, I have read *Nymphs* by Ernest Schwiebert, published in 1973.

Leafing through the pages of this book and admiring the beautiful, color plates of various nymphs, enlarged four times, I came across the plates illustrating the caddis pupae. I was struck by what I saw . . . the green, gold, yellow, brown, and orange of the slender bodies, the small drooping wings, and the long floppy, hanging legs extending beyond the ends of the bodies! "These are softhackles," I thought.

Hungrily, I read through the three chapters on the caddis and microcaddis. Schwiebert said there were hunreds of species of the insects and that they were to be found just about anywhere. He believed them to be the "most numerous of the aquatic insects extant in American trout water, making their availability factor relatively high."

In this observation, Schwiebert agreed with J.R. Harris, whose book *An Angler's Entomology* was first published in England in 1952. Harris writes that:

> Caddis-flies, Sedge-flies, or as they are often called in Ireland, Rails, form numerically the largest of the three main groups of water flies. They belong to the order Trichoptera.
> ... Caddis-flies differ widely in their development from both stone flies and ephemeroptans in one obvious respect. The two latter orders pass from the egg to a larval stage and then to a winged stage. But caddis-flies pass from the egg to the larval and then through a pupal stage before they assume a winged form.

Not only were there more of them (caddis flies), Schwiebert said, but they were also more hardy than the mayfly class and less susceptible to pollution and pesticides. He also hinted that the caddis is better fished as a shallow sunk fly than as a dry, because the dry was difficult to imitate as a fluttering insect on or above the water and that it was easier to imitate the swimming pupae, which were more easily caught by the trout.

Almost all of the artificial caddis pupae in his chapters are tied with partridge, grouse, and similar bird, soft-hackles. Mr. Schwiebert pays homage to the earlier British, and British North Country angling writers who wrote about them more than one hundred years ago.

After seeing his paintings of the caddis pupae and read-

A stretch of the Pere Marquette near Baldwin, Michigan.

ing his clear and sane sentences about them, I knew I had to amend my own thinking about what the soft-hackled flies do, in fact, imitate and to feel grateful that Schwiebert came to write a book like that.

Ephemera or Trichoptera? Or both?

With so many different mayfly nymphs and their duns, and with so many different caddis pupae in the water at the same time, it seems impossible to imitate any specific one when fishing the sunk fly. This is why I have never used or believed in the hard bodied nymphs, the flattened imitations or rubber molded ones. Any attempt to imitate any specific nymph or dun, would seem to limit the appeal to the trout by the exact imitation. This is the basic difference between dry fly fishing and sunk fly fishing. It is a very different kind of ball game. Fishing on top, the angler wants the exact imitation because he can see what fly is up. Fishing under the surface, the angler wants the barest resemblance to the dozens of different kinds of nymphs or pupae, because he can never see or know what is really happening down there. Any sunk artificial fly, to be good, must transform itself in the water into something alive, something suggestive and moving, something that looks good to eat. Such a fly looks different in the water than it does out of it. The best way to demonstrate this is to look at the soft-hackled fly dry, then wet it and take another look.

The transformation is amazing!

The soft partridge or snipe or starling feathers with their tapered barbs, mold themselves against the body with the tips away and toward the tail of the fly. There is a natural lump or thorax created at the front of the fly, by reason of the tapering of the barbs, the thicker part being closer to the stem of the feather.

As the fly floats downstream, these barbs close in and out, squirm against the body of the fly, and react in a lifelike way to every little kind of pressure.

Without wings, the fly has no top or bottom, and will look the same to the fish no matter what side is up. Frequently, a trout caught on the fly will have the hook in his top lip with the bend pointed up instead of down.

The soft-hackled fly also can be described as not a nymph still, not a dun yet; not a pupae still, not an adult caddis yet. The hackle barbs are really too long and too soft and too many to represent the six legs of the nymph. The barbs could suggest dun wings just as they are cracking open during emergence or, taken for the caddis pupae, they definitely could suggest the longer legs and drooping wings. They might even suggest the mature fly, fluttering on the surface.

On any soft-hackled fly it is obvious, however, that the hackle is everything. It must do all the work to make the fly so successful. To prove or disprove this, some day, I'm going to fish the fly with hackle only, but the reader will have to wait to hear the results of that experiment.

Chapter VI

One gets a particular delight in finding in angling literature a mention of his peculiar way of fishing; his favorite fly or group of flies; his most beloved river; or anything about the subject of fly fishing especially akin to him. The more often one sees the reference, the more one knows he is on the right track himself. He can say, "See, so and so has said it and it must be right." The older the literary reference, the more excited and elated is the beholder. The more revered or popular or championed is the writer, the more convinced is the reader. The search for agreement is at work and it is true not only in fishing, but in other sports, as well.

When I first started fishing the soft-hackled fly, I didn't know what deep and opulent water I was wading in. First, I thought Young had invented the fly. He after all, already was credited with the invention of the Strawman nymph and the midge rod. But no one invents flies or styles; they are evolved, developed, borrowed, adopted, adapted or stolen. I know that now, because from the earliest known work on angling to some of the most recent, there is frequent mention, yes, even whole books, of and on the soft-hackled fly.

In fact, a search reveals so much mention and attention to it, that I have been puzzled why this small group of flies hasn't prospered more in America, especially since we are a country of predominantly wet fly fishers.

Besides the mention found in *Nymphs,* by Ernest Schwiebert, already shown in the last chapter, the other newest reference is found in *Quill Gordon,* by John McDonald, published in 1972. Here I learned of the oldest reference, found in *The Treatise of Fishing with an Angle,* by the Prioress of Sopwell Convent, Dame Juliana Berners, and dated 1496. Through some of the most assiduous angling research I have ever encountered, McDonald takes apart the twelve flies described in the *Treatise,* unscrambles the Middle English of the period and recreates the flies so that they can then be illustrated in his beautiful book.

He says:

> In the present stage of knowledge, secure conclusions cannot be made on several critical points. In instances where it is impossible to render a logically strong judgement between choices, we present our first choice as the most likely, and alternatives as possible but less likely. The alternatives are offered in the illustrations and the table of our dressings.
>
> Now look at the flies and our argument for the dressing of each.

Using the language of the treatise, he describes the first

fly in the list, "The donne flye, the body of the donne wool and the wings of the pertryche [*partridge*]." He asks the first question: does "dun" imply an insect or color or material? He thinks it a color. He asks the second question: was the partridge a wing or body feather? He thinks it a wing feather. He asks the third question: was the feather hackled round the hook or tied upright? He thinks it unhackled.

His second alternative shows a fly very similar to my own partridge hackled flies, and this makes me feel good. Because of my interest in the soft-hackle, I might argue that it should be the first choice. But I don't.

Here's why. When I saw the first trout flies in Glen Buckel's barber shop window and later when I tried to tie the same flies, I thought the hackle barbs were tied in under and around the hook individually or in small groups of individual barbs. Needless to say, it was impossible to make them stand straight out like they did on Glen's flies. I had read no books and received no instruction, so I didn't know the barbs splayed out as the hackle was wound around the shank of the hook. One day soon after, Glen was showing me some very nice hackles and wound one around his finger. It was like magic, the light went on as the separate barbs spread round and round his finger.

So it is possible that Berners was as ignorant as I and didn't grasp this amazing characteristic of a simple hackle, even though there were earlier "books of credence" which might have told her exactly about the proper way of handling the hackle.

John Waller Hills, the famous angling historian, thought differently, however. In his *A History of Fly Fishing For Trout* first published in 1921, he endowed the Dame with more knowledge than I do. Hills believed the first fly of her list, the Donne Fly, to be exactly the same as the Partridge and Orange as it is dressed in England today, as it was dressed by Paul Young in Michigan and as it is dressed in this book. Hills thought the fly to be an imitation of the February Red, a stonefly. He says:

> February Red. This is the *Treatise's* "dun fly, the body of dun wool and the wings of the partridge". That is the dressing in 1496. It is the same today. The Partridge and Orange, dressed with a partridge hackle and a body of orange silk, is the imitation most commonly used between the Tweed and the Trent and kills hundreds of trout every year. So that fly has not changed at all in four centuries and a quarter. There have, of course, been innumerable dressings during the period, and the fly has been given various names. Markham called it the Lesser Dun Fly, dressed with dun wool and the partridge hackle; and Cotton the Red Brown, dressed with a body of red-brown dog's fur and wings of light mallard. Chetham, not in his book but in the remarkable list of flies in the appendix, calls it the Prime Dun, with a body of fox cub's down spun on ash-coloured silk and wings from a starling's quill feather. Bowlker called it the Red Fly, and dressed it with a red squirrel's fur body, a red hackle and dark mallard wings. Aldam, exactly like the *Treatise,* mahogany silk and partridge hackle. And so on, to modern times, when it is dressed with a body of orange silk and hackled either with partridge, grouse, or woodcock, according to the fancy of the writer. It is the same fly throughout. There can be no doubt about the identification. It is the first fly given in the list in the *Treatise* and it is the first fly which greets the fisherman when the inhospitable winter is over. The earliest French list also gives a fly not dissimilar

for the month of April: body of red silk, head green, and wings from a red hen.

In the same chapter of this book, Hills divided the work of all fly tiers and fly fishing writers into three groups: "fancy flies," "general flies," and "actual copy." He says:

> Of course these three schools merge into each other. A fly can be more or less general, or it can be on the borderland of fancy and general, or of general and individual. Take the Partridge and Orange as an example. It is fished in the north all the year round, and may be called a fancy fly. But it is possibly the best imitation of the February Red, and when so used it is specific. And besides the February Red, it also kills as an imitation of the nymph of the Blue Winged Olive, and as such is general.

Describing further the characteristics of the "fancy flies," Hills says:

> They have many redoubtable advocates, drawn in modern times chiefly from Scotland. Stewart pinned his faith to his three famous hackles, his black, red and dun spider. No doubt each of those could, with a little laxity, be identified with a specific insect; but he did not set out to imitate such, and chose his flies with an eye rather to weather and water. This, in fact, is the feature which distinguished this school: more attention is paid to light, to the clearness of the water, and to the sky, than to the insect. Stewart has many followers to this day.

It is quite possible the first soft-hackled fly was used in

America around 1832, not by an American, but by an Englishman. In *The Angler's Souvenir*, P. Fisher, Esq., London, 1835, the author and two fishing pals are imbibing ale, sherry, and port at the Rye-House in London. Under the influence of so potent an alcohol combination, their conversations might not be taken too seriously.

SIMPSON: Have you ever seen any American books on angling, Fisher?

FISHER: No, I do not think there are any published. Brother Jonathon is not yet sufficiently civilized to produce anything original on the art. There is good trout fishing in America, and the streams which are all free, are much less fished than in our Island, "from the small number of gentlemen," as an American writer says, "who are at leisure to give their time to it".

And later.

SIMPSON: A gentleman of the name of Vigne, a member of Lincoln's Inn, took a trip to America about three years ago, during the long vacation, and enjoyed a few days' fly-fishing in Pennsylvania. He had some fair sport in the Juniata, one of the tributaries of the Susquehannah. The trout were from half a pound to three pounds in weight; and in a little more than two hours' fishing he caught about six dozen. He mentions the red-hackle as the best fly that an angler can throw in Spring Creek.

FISHER: The red-hackle is deadly on all waters, though not at all times. It is one of my three types for the colour of flies. The red, black, and grouse hackle are with me standards.

The red hackle, as dressed then, must have been a red cock's hackle with an orange silk body. It could have been the Partridge and Orange because the fly has been known by many other names in the past, as we have already seen. But dare I assume, since the grouse hackle was standard with one of these gentlemen, it might not have been tried by the one fortunate enough to visit America during that time.

In 1857, W.C. Stewart, a Scot, had published his book, *The Practical Angler*. Only seventy-three pages of the more than 200 in the book deal with fly fishing and they are devoted almost exclusively to just three soft-hackled flies (or spiders as the author calls them) and how to fish them.

The seventy-three pages must be packed with piscatorial dynamite for they have led some fishing writers to call Stewart the fourth most influential author in the history of angling. The same pages have helped the book become a classic in angling literature, which had been printed and reprinted nineteen times by 1961.

I don't know if the book is much read in America. The spiders are described in *The Fly and the Fish*, John Atherton, 1951, and in *The Art of Tying the Wet Fly*, James E. Leisenring and Vernon S. Hidy, 1941.

Stewart's three spiders are practically hackle-only flies. The first is the Black Spider, a little brown tying-silk on the shank and a small starling feather wound at the head and down slightly toward (palmered) the bend. The second is the Red Spider, a little yellow silk on the shank and a small feather taken from the outside of the wing of the landrail. The third is the Dun Spider, with no mention by Stewart of the tying silk, or body, but with the specification of a soft dun or ash colored feather taken from the outside of the wing of the dotteral. A small feather can be substituted from the inside of the wing of the starling.

(Many other writers have noticed the lack of the mention of a body material or color on the Dun Spider. Their inference has been that the silk was left out through a printing error. I believe Stewart never intended this fly to have any body at all, but meant it to become the first hackle-only fly in history.)

Stewart loved and praised similar hackles; mavis, grey plover, golden plover, partridge, and grouse. He said:

> Their superiority consists in their much greater resemblance to the legs of an insect, and their extreme softness. So soft are they, that when a spider is made of one of them and placed in the water, the least motion will agitate and impart a singularly lifelike appearance to it, whereas it would have no effect upon a cock's hackle.

The reference to the legs of the insect by Stewart is interesting, because it runs contrary to modern thinking which seems to place emphasis on body and wings.

Stewart knew the value of the natural float and was one of the first writers to advocate fly fishing upstream. He admonishes the downstream angler who casts his fly or flies across stream and drags them to his bank, the fly or flies having, "the strength and agility of an otter."

Later:

> In addition to drawing their flies across the stream, some anglers practice what is called playing their flies, which is done by a jerking motion of the wrist, which imparts a similar motion to the fly. Their object in doing this is to create an ap-

pearance of life, and thus render their flies more attractive. An appearance of life is certainly a great temptation to a trout, but it may be much better accomplished by dressing the flies of soft materials, which the water can agitate, and thus create a natural motion of the legs or wings of the fly, than by dragging them by jumps of a foot at a time across and up a roaring stream. Trout are not accustomed to see small insects making such gigantic efforts at escape, and therefore it is calculated to awaken their suspicions.

Had mending been invented by Stewart's time I'm sure he would have taken to it, because he does admit that fishing upstream is more physically difficult, harder to learn successfully, and "requires more nicety in casting."

Heading toward a verbal confrontation with the growing "exact imitation school" of fly fishermen situated in England, particularly in the south, Stewart says:

Those anglers who think trout will take no fly unless it is an exact imitation of some one of the immense number of flies they are feeding on, must suppose that they know to a shade the color of every fly on the water, and can detect the least deviation from it—an amount of entomological knowledge that would put to shame the angler himself, and a good many naturalists to boot.

More important to Stewart, than color and exact imitation, were shape and "extreme lightness and neatness of form." And in the same paragraph:

Every possible advantage is in favour of a lightly dressed fly; it is more like a natural insect; it falls lighter on the water, and every angler knows the importance of making his fly fall gently, and there being less material about it, the artificial nature of that material is not so easily detected; and also, as the hook is not so much covered with feathers, there is a much better chance of hooking a trout when it rises.

Stewart was no tongue-in-cheek writer. He said what he wanted to say and meant it, with a slight hint of command in all of his instructions on fly fishing and fly tying. There was something of the braggadocio in him, too, especially due to the large bags of trout he and his flies and his methods were reportedly sure to take.

When Francis Francis, a fine and popular angler-writer of the time, intimated that Scottish trout and Scottish fishermen were not as smart as the British, Stewart, the proud Scot retorts:

If Mr. Francis' views as to an exact imitation being necessary in English streams be correct, which we very much doubt, he will require to find some other reason for its being unnecessary in Scotland than this. In comparing the severity of the fishing in Scotch and English streams, it must be borne in mind that the former are, as a rule, open to the public, and that the latter, as a rule, are preserved, and fished only by a favoured few.

We repudiate with scorn the bare idea that it requires less skill to catch a Scotch trout than an English one, or that the former in any way receives an inferior education as regards flies, etc., to his English Brother.

If Francis and Stewart did not agree on the relative sophistication of the British trout and fishermen and Scottish trout and fishermen, they did agree on the direction to take once they were in the stream. And Francis pays compliment to Stewart by including his spiders in the section, "General Flies," in his own work, *A Book on Angling*, issued in 1867.

Francis also included the Grouse Hackle and Partridge Hackle in his general flies and said, "The last two flies will fill a basket on any mountain beck or trout burn in heather districts."

The older literary work most akin to this present one has to be T.E. Pritt's, *Yorkshire Trout Flies*, from 1885. In it, he has listed sixty-two wet fly patterns, most of them without wings and with hackles from the wings and bodies of such birds as golden plovers, dotterel, starling, woodcock, grouse, water hen, snipe, partridge, pheasants, and jackdaws.

His "Number 28" fly had a body of yellow silk and a light feather from the back of a partridge for a hackle. His description of the fly reads, "a good killer almost any time during April." Number 32 is the Orange Partridge, the same as Number 28 but with an orange silk body. "These are practically the same flies and are very excellent killers."

Most of the flies in this book are also included in Pritt's work, except for the thorax models, including the Tups, which are described in a later chapter.

In another, later (1896) and not so popular book, *An Angler's Basket*, Pritt gives his reason for his preference of the wingless fly:

> A hackled fly, as we dress it in the north, makes no attempt to imitate the shape of the winged insect; but if you will take

a living fly and dip it under water you will find that, in all but the very strongly-winged flies, the shape goes irrevocably, though the color and size remain, and it is to these two points that the fly dresser's attention should be directed in dressing flies for all rapid streams.

So it appears, the soft-hackles were used extensively in Scotland and the border waters of the British Isles. "The stamp of origin is there, clearly recognizable to any student of trout flies," says W.H. Lawrie, in *Scottish Trout Flies,* 1966.

Deliberate restraint in the use of materials, the short, slender bodies, sparse hackle, spare wings, and a preference for the sober hues of nature, all accord with a national tradition in respect of frugality and modesty.
 . . . traditionally, the trout fisher north of the border has always been concerned with the wet fly . . . the aim then was to simulate living insects—hatching flies, drowning flies, nymphs and larvae—in form, colour and size, and to do so in such a way that the representations would be readily submersible and swim well in the tumbling waters of fast-flowing rivers. It is this quality of submersibility which has governed trout-fly designs in Scotland as far back as can be traced.

Later:

The popular explanation offered to account for the hackled fly's comparative success in hard-fished waters is generally that it is much more lightly dressed than a winged pattern, and that, in consequence, trout are less likely to detect its artificiality.

If I have established some kind of origin for the soft-hackled fly, I should add that the early fishing Scots and Yorkshiremen were not well-heeled gentlemen. According to Lawrie, they had to work for a living, and fish after the working was done. They observed the Sabbath, a custom still practiced on much Scottish water. It seems natural that these country fellows would use flies which were simple and cheap to make, of which the soft-hackles are. I imagine most of the Scottish "locals" shot their own partridge and grouse and woodcock. Wings on flies have always been tricky to fly tiers, and if these fishing gentlemen thought the flies would catch fish without them, they would just as soon leave them off.

But what of the water where these flies prevailed and are still used today? Here is one description from the Lonsdale Library, Volume II, *Trout Fishing from All Angles*, Eric Tavener, 1933.

> The typical hill-stream is made up of fast and broken water relieved by stretches where the current flows less rapidly and by smooth glides. Such are to be found in Yorkshire, Devonshire, Wales, Scotland and elsewhere. The character of the rivers is for the most part rocky, the upper parts are boulder-strewn and the pace is often too rapid to allow the hatching duns time to mature for flight before they are drowned in the rough waters of the stickles. Although insects, water-bred and wind-borne, are plentiful, the duns which are able to ride out the rough water are not very numerous nor are the opportunities of using the dry fly.

During the nineteenth century, before the concrete codification of the use of the dry fly, the soft-hackled fly was not only popular in Scotland and border country, but also very much used all over England. A 1967 reference work by Lawrie, *English Trout Flies,* shows that from more than twenty fly-fishing authors of the 1800's, sixteen of them included the Grouse Hackle and Partridge Hackle in their lists of the most killing patterns. One author liked the fly so well, he tied it with eleven different colored bodies.

Why was the soft-hackled fly so popular in England during the nineteenth century and why did the style lose favor in the current century? At that time, we here in America were imitating British fishing styles and importing British flies and tackle, so why didn't the soft-hackled fly make it to these shores in more numbers than it did?

The answer may be found in the writings of F.M. Halford. In two books, *Floating Flies and How to Dress Them* (1886), and *Dry-Fly Fishing in Theory and Practice* (1889), Halford laid down the cornerstone of the exact imitation school of dry fly fishing.

About the dry fly and everything Halford stood for, J.W. Hills, in *A Summer on the Test* (1924), said:

> Wherever it (the dry fly) was introduced, it conquered. The sunkfly was swept away, beaten and ridiculed.
> . . . everyone thought it would rule forever. Its advantages are so obvious. Its imaginative appeal is so powerful.

Under Halford's code, the fly fisherman cast only to a rising fish with a fly that was supposed to be the exact imitation, in color, size, and form, of the natural insect the trout had just taken. And the imitation had to float high and dry, with wings cocked, and to float without drag. The fly patterns were beautiful with rare, glossy cock hackles in all shades of dun from light honey to dark blue andalusian and with bodies made up mostly of stripped quills or silk floss. There was considerable dyeing, too, of hackles, wings and body materials in no less than nine special dyes, in the attempt to match the subtle hues of the chalk stream ephemera.

Halford's system and philosophy, although developed for the gin-clear, slow gliding waters of the south of England, spread to the more turbulent and rambling rivers of the north and Scotland. Then they took a longer, western trip to the United States. One of the first fly fishermen here to respond to the new wave was Theodore Gordon, later called, "The Halford of the U.S.A." In 1890, after writing to Halford, Gordon received a sampling of the exact imitation dry flies.

He found they were not suited to our eastern trout streams; first in their inability to ride the rougher waters and second, they imitated no real native insects.

In setting out to establish artificial flies which did resemble our own eastern water-borne insects, Gordon developed both the Gordon and the Quill Gordon. But even these flies imitate not one, but a large number of flies which are found on the Beaverkill, the Au Sable, and Madison Rivers.

Interestingly enough, however, one fly in Gordon's final list, aptly named, "Quite Killing," has no wings but just a partridge hackle wound over a light bluish dun body of fur or wool.

With Gordon, America was definitely on the dry fly bandwagon. Other fishing writers jumped on: George La Branche, *The Dry Fly and Fast Water;* Emlyn M. Gill, *Practical*

Dry-Fly Fishing; and later Preston Jennings, Vincent C. Marinaro, and Art Flick. By 1938, the soft-hackled fly was almost unheard of in this country. That year, Ray Bergman published, *Trout,* an encyclopedic type of book, encompassing every known way to catch them, considered by many to be the "bible" for trout fishermen for years to come. The book contains plate after plate of heavily painted flies, all in a row, with wings prettily set. Of 385 wet flies shown and eighteen- or twenty-odd nymphs, only one, the Grouse Spider, even came close to the sober soft-hackled flies of Stewart and Pritt. Bergman's dressing called for either an orange floss or chenille body and a disgracing, long crimson tail.

In addition to Schwiebert's *Nymphs,* only one other American fishing writer has touched on the soft-hackled fly in a book; *The Art of Tying the Wet Fly* (1941), by James E. Leisenring. It could have been the fact of war-time which prevented the book from becoming more widely known, but in any case, even though I started collecting fly fishing literature some time ago, I didn't know of the book until it was re-published in 1971. Leisenring apparently admired the soft-hackles, although some of his flies do include wings. He was supposed to have a reputation for catching more and bigger fish than anyone else on the Pennsylvania Brodheads Creek and elsewhere, but because of the lack of that kind of information in his book, how he did it remained his secret.

I should also give "mending" credit to John Atherton who wrote *The Fly and the Fish* (1951). Probably because Atherton was an avid salmon fisherman (he died on the banks of one of the great Maritime rivers), he had heard or read of greased line fishing and possibly even used the method for salmon and, as he says he did, in wet fly fishing for trout.

> The usual wet-fly technique is pretty much a cut-and-dried affair. The angler casts his fly across, or across and downstream, and lets it swing around in the current, sometimes with movement imparted, sometimes "dead." In fishing with a tight line in this manner, the fly is apt to move too rapidly. For usually, after the cast is made, the pull of the current on the line and leader causes a downstream belly in the line. Then the fly is pulled downstream and whipped around in a manner resembling scarcely at all the action of underwater insect life.
> ... To bring the fly slowly to the fish is a different matter entirely and requires a different method. If the angler can control the speed of his fly by the cast and the subsequent manipulation of rod and line, he has already made possible a more lifelike presentation. Fishing in the manner of greased-line salmon fishing, the line is cast across current or up and across, with enough slack to allow a free drift for some distance. This method has been described often but the reasons for its effectiveness have seldom been mentioned. It is not only the natural movement of the fly but the view of the fly by the fish that is greatly responsible for its success. For the fly is more apt to drift sideways in the current and the trout sees it from the side, where it is not only more noticeable but more attractive.

Just as Halford's dry-fly-only doctrine marched north and to America, the appeal and efficiency of the soft-hackle moved south right into the bastion of the dry fly cult. Disgruntled angler-writers like Skues and John Waller Hills, both famous chalkstream men and early disciples of Halford, took to it with avidity once the sunken fly was no longer prohibited on chalkstream waters.

Skues, in search of wet fly designs and styles, turned to a Scot, David Webster in *The Angler and the Loop Rod* (1885). These were mostly winged patterns, but Skues says, in *The Way of a Trout with a Fly:*

> A soft-hackled fly adjusts itself easily to the action of the water, but a fly with stiff, staring, upright wings or hackles may easily cause such a disturbance in the water as to give proof of a bad entry. The lines, therefore, on which an artificial wet fly that is to be fishing against the stream in any way is built ought to be fine, like the lines of a yacht or swift boat, or high class motor, sloping backwards, so as to offer the least possible resistance to the current, and such resistance as there is should be elastic. The fly ought to be equal on both sides, so as to balance accurately and to swim smoothly, and any excess of bulk is to be deprecated.

Remember my earlier comment on the soft-hackled fly having no top or bottom!

In another book, *Minor Tactics of the Chalk Stream* (Second Edition, 1914), Skues discusses the problems facing the dry fly angler, when a cross stream wind drives the natural floaters to the far bank, "into little pools and eddies between the prominences on that bank, and so out of the line of the current which would otherwise carry them along." The picture he paints here is a difficult one for a natural drag-free float with the imitation. The fish are feeding in what might be perfectly called still water yet are separated from the angler by the main current of the river. The only chance he will have, says Skues, "is to hit your fish with it (the dry fly) on the tip of the nose at a moment when few naturals are about."

Skues says this is the occasion for the spare-hackled wet fly.

> The advantage which the wet fly has is not that the trout is taking the nymph in preference to the floating dun, though he is probably doing that far more than is apparent, but that, whereas a drag on the surface is fatal and betrays the gut, an underwater drag is not betraying, and the movement of the fly caused by the drag, may, in its beginning at any rate, be even attractive to the trout, as imparting motion suggesting life and volition to an otherwise suspicious object. The drag also serves to tighten instead of slackening the line, so that a very small strike fixes the hook.

Missing the fish through striking in this manner will not scare and put down the fish, Skues says, but, "where a strike with a floating fly would send him headlong to cover."

To illustrate the problem and solution, Skues picks a day in July, 1908.

> A few little pale duns were going down, being beaten by the wind into and among the bays along the opposite bank. . .
>
> Three trout, and three only, could I find moving, and they were taking every dun which went over them.

Skues put all three fish down with various dry flies:

> I put up as an experiment a tiny dotterel hackle tied with

primrose tying silk in the true Stewart style, not with the fibres radiating from the head, but palmer-wise for halfway down the body. The trout had it at the very first offer, and was duly landed. I went to the next, and got him almost immediately. The third, for some reason, had no use for Dotterel duns, but the moment I covered him with a Tups Indispensable he slashed it, and joined the other two in my creel.

The most interesting part of the foregoing, as pertaining to the soft-hackled fly, is the observation, so typically Skues, that underwater drag is not detrimental, but, indeed, beneficial to catching trout feeding on dries or nymphs or pupae. For this kind of angling reasoning and logic and enjoyment, Skues had been, only a few years before, ridiculed by many staunch Halford disciples, and on some water, it has been said, even barred from fishing in such a disgraceful manner.

Behind Skues and along with him (for they were contemporaries) comes John Waller Hills with the most convincing testimony for the soft-hackled fly, I have found anywhere.

Hills says he first fished the Test around 1888. In *A Summer on the Test,* first published in 1924, we find him on that "noble river" during the whole fishing season of the same year. How much or how often he fished the Test between 1888 and 1924, I cannot say, but I would presume it would have been for enough seasons for him to have known and to have followed personally, the dry-fly-only rules that prevailed there during the earlier years.

At any rate, there is very little, if any, mention made of sunk fly fishing on the Test in his first edition. Six years later, in 1930, Hills wrote the second edition, and included ten new chapters, one of which was on the nymph. The testimony for the soft-hackled fly is to be found here.

> One of the softest, most compressible, patterns is the Partridge Hackle, and, whether this be the reason or not, I consider it the best sunk fly on the Test. Its body, of silk, can be of many colours. I find the old Cumberland pattern, the Orange Partridge, best; and next to that the red.

In a later book, *River Keeper* (1934), the story of William James Lunn, keeper of the water on the Test belonging to the Houghton Club, Hills tells of Lunn's experience with the soft-hackle.

> If anglers will cast their minds back they will recall that by 1917 both small spent spinners and under-water flies were well established: Mr. Skues had written Minor tactics in 1910, and Halford had dressed spent spinners. So naturally Lunn next turned his attention to sunk patterns, and over a series of years he evolved his well-known partridge hackles. He did not invent this pattern; it is a very old north country fly and is actually mentioned in the year 1496 in the earliest list of flies in English. I do not know who brought partridge hackles to the Test: I, who had long known the partridge-and-orange on the Cumberland Eden, brought it to the Kennet in about the year 1912, but did not do much with it. It became firmly established at Stockbridge, and spread thence to many waters. It kills either floating, or awash, or sunk. However, let me go back to Lunn's share in its evolution. In 1916 he dressed the little red partridge hackle, No. 8 in the list, with a body of dark red silk, on a 000 hook (size 17): this, like the orange partridge, was a well-known pattern in common use in York-

shire, but unknown, I believe, on the Test. This was the only partridge hackle tried for seven years: but in 1923 Lunn brought out his very good big orange partridge, No. 7, a different pattern with a different appeal. It has a body of bright orange artificial silk, ribbed with gold wire, and, like all its tribe, it is hackled at the head only; tie it on a large hook, Lunn says No. 1, (size 14), but I have used it up to No. 2 or 3, (sizes 13 or 12). It is invaluable for both trout and grayling, in all weathers and waters. I regard it as specially potent when you have risen but not pricked a fish on some imitation of the olive. But I have also known it taken by fish obviously smutting in still water on a breathless day. Those two, the little red partridge dressed very small, and the large orange dressed very big, are the best by far of all the partridges. Nor have I done much (though other anglers have) with Lunn's little yellow or little green partridge, Nos. 10 and 9 in the list, both tied on 000 hooks, also invented in 1923. Lunn considers they do well on those hot July days when trout are taking something which you cannot see.

The partridge hackle of one kind or another is much the best under-water fly at Stockbridge, better than any other sunk fly or nymph. In fact, I believe it kills more than all under-water patterns put together. It has one immense advantage; being small and composed of a soft feather, it is easy to suck in. Lunn considers this very important. Trout, especially as the season gets on and they become fat and lazy, hardly open their mouths when taking a fly either real or unreal. They draw in a thread of water, the fly with it, expelling the water through their gills and retaining the fly. Once, watching a trout being fished for on a hot day in slow water, Lunn saw it attempt to suck in the angler's artificial, but fail to get it into its mouth as the fly did not pass its hardly opened lips. Without moving, Lunn called out to the fisherman to put on a little red partridge, and had the satisfaction of seeing this quietly drawn in and the trout hooked and landed. For myself I believe that far too little attention is paid to softness of fibre and general collapsibility of a fly. When we miss or only scratch a fish on a mayfly tied with a feather with a stiff rib, this may be the cause. And certainly I hook better with the modern soft-hackles than with the cock's feathers which were thought essential in the early days of the dry fly, and I fancy this difference exists even with the smallest 000 patterns.

Halford, himself, had something amazingly good to say about the soft-hackled fly. He was a firm believer, as have been many other fishermen before and after him, in autopsy to determine the trout's diet. In a chapter on the subject in *Dry-Fly Fishing in Theory and Practice,* he says:

> It has already been shown that by far the larger proportion of the contents of the stomach of a trout or grayling consists of larvae, nymphae, caddis, shrimps, &c., which are invariably in the middle and lower depths of the water, from which fact the inference must be drawn that the major part of their food is taken below the surface. At the first glance, a natural deduction from this would be, that the sunk fly would be more likely to tempt than the floating one. Very possibly many of the sparsely dressed patterns used more generally in the north for wet-fly fishing are taken for some forms of larvae, or even in some cases water-beetles, and it has been confidently said by north country anglers of great experience, that an adept of their style could work sad havoc on some of the well-stocked shallows of the chalkstreams.

Chapter VII

It is very interesting to note that in *The Fisherman's Handbook of Trout Flies* (1960), by Donald DuBois, the soft partridge hackle is only the fifteenth most common hackle to be used of the 5939 patterns listed in that book. The grouse hackle is even lower. Both hackles are very near the bottom of the list.

The partridge hackle is called for in eighty-two patterns in the book, some of them including wings. The infrequency of the use of the partridge and other soft, game bird hackles, means, of course, the material is unpopular to fly tiers and to fly fishermen. I have shown, however, that before the development of the dry fly, these hackles were of the most popular on English and Scottish rivers.

The hackles are not hard to come by. Most fly tying material houses sell them, and they are very inexpensive compared to fancy rooster hackles. The amateur fly tier can almost always find a hunting friend who might supply him with these feathers from the birds shot during a hunt.

Since you will not be able to purchase freely many of the soft-hackled flies in this book, it is recommended that you tie your own. If you have never tied flies before, I urge you to start immediately. The practice is exhilarating. It is romantic. It lifts you up when you are depressed and downhearted. That it gives joy and pleasure is confirmed by the fact that some hospitals now encourage fly tying as a form of therapy. There is no closed season and the worse the weather outside, the better and more exciting is the task inside.

Once you fall for it, you will never be without pictures of the hackles, silks, tinsels, furs, colored threads and finished flies in your mind and in your heart, and you will feel much the better for it. It is one of the few good things left to do by oneself, alone, in our present world of rush hours, deadlines, and group participation and activity.

For me, the art of tying is much like love. Frequently, when I haven't tied flies for some time, I am drawn by a tremendous urge to return to the table; first to look at the materials, then to feel them and then to create a new fly or make one of the old, familiar patterns. I even carry the art with me in a plastic sewing box during my photographic assignments to St. Louis, Birmingham, Detroit or wherever.

Anyone can do it. A couple of years ago I met a construction worker who wanted to take up fly fishing and fly tying. He had worked for many years as a mason and had hands like hams. I was sure that he would be my most difficult pupil, that he would tear the silks and soft hackles apart before he could get them on the hook. Don't you believe it. The first evening, he was tying the simple partridge flies by himself. They looked fine and well proportioned. And they certainly would catch trout.

The equipment needs for tying soft-hackles are small: a vise, scissors, an old hat pin, or new bodkin, a thread bobbin, and a rubber tipped hackle-pliers.

The material list includes: partridge hackles (brown and gray), grouse hackles, woodcock hackles, jackdaw neck, starling hackles and wings, snipe wings, narrow gold and silver tinsels, hooks, orange, yellow, green and purple silk floss; orange, yellow, green and red tying silk; hare's ears and mask, mole fur, peacock herl, blue dun hen hackles, center tail of common rooster pheasant, thin copper wire, head cement and liquid wax. You may also add pink fur or wool.

On page 97 of this book are shown fourteen different soft-hackled flies. These are the ones I have used, but there are many more in angling literature, or you might mix colors and materials for experimenting on your own.

Here are the recipes for the fourteen flies. Hook sizes 10-16.

1. PARTRIDGE AND ORANGE
   body: Orange silk floss
   hackle: Brown partridge

2. PARTRIDGE AND GREEN
   body: Green silk floss
   hackle: Gray partridge

3. PARTRIDGE AND YELLOW
   body: Yellow silk floss
   hackle: Brown or gray partridge

76 THE SOFT-HACKLED FLY

4. PARTRIDGE AND ORANGE AND FUR THORAX
    body: 2/3's, orange silk floss
    thorax: Black and brown hare's face
    hackle: Brown partridge

5. PARTRIDGE AND GREEN AND FUR THORAX
    body: 2/3's, green silk floss
    thorax: Black and brown hare's face
    hackle: Gray partridge

6. PARTRIDGE AND YELLOW AND FUR THORAX
    body: 2/3's yellow silk floss
    thorax: Light brown hare's face
    hackle: Brown or gray partridge

7. TUPS INDISPENSABLE
    body: 2/3's, yellow silk floss
    thorax: light pink
    tail: four or five whisks blue dun hen
    hackle: Blue dun hen (This is an often-used British pattern.) With a cock blue dun hackle, the fly is fished dry as a spinner. It is the only pattern in the book calling for poultry hackle. I have often thought it would be a better soft-hackled fly if the hackle were dyed blue dun partridge, for more mobility and compressibility. The thorax design of this fly led me to develop my own partridge and thorax patterns, although Skues mentions having fished similar flies in *The Way of a Trout with a Fly*. The Tups and the thorax patterns are obviously more meaty than the plain floss bodies, and sometimes will seem more effective.

8. IRON BLUE DUN
    tail: Four or five whisks white hen hackle

tag: Red tying silk
body: Mole's fur spun on the red tying silk
hackle: Very short jackdaw

9. SNIPE AND PURPLE

    body: Purple silk floss

    hackle: Small covert hackle from snipe wing (these are the very short feathers on the leading edge of the wings).

10. PHEASANT TAIL

    body: Four or five of the longest herls of the center tail of a rooster pheasant wound on together with very thin copper wire.

    hackle: Brown or gray partridge

    tail: 2 or 3 whisks from the center tail feather of a rooster pheasant. This fly is very common in England today, and when a Britisher says he is nymph fishing, he generally means he is fishing the pheasant tail only. There, however, the pattern does not use any hackle, but the thorax is built up with continued winding of the pheasant herls and copper wire. Some British tyers use the copper wire as the tying thread. The thin copper wire is not available from any fly tying material house I know of, but can be obtained from any small appliance repair shop.

11. SNIPE AND YELLOW

    body: Yellow silk floss

    hackle: Small covert hackle from snipe wing

12. MARCH BROWN SPIDER

    body: Mixed hair from hare's face
    rib: Narrow gold
    hackle: Brown partridge
    tying silk: Orange

78 THE SOFT-HACKLED FLY

13. GROUSE AND ORANGE
    body: Orange silk floss
    hackle: Black and orange grouse hackle. (It is very difficult to tell the difference between the grouse hackle and the woodcock hackle. They are both black and orange barred and either one could substitute for the other.)

14. STARLING AND HERL
    body: Peacock herl
    hackle: Small covert hackle from starling wing

The green, yellow and orange bodies are the more popular colors used in the soft-hackled flies. But the patterns are listed in fly fishing literature with practically every color imaginable, as has already been pointed out.

The bodies of these flies are very slim, the floss just barely covering the hook shank. In the smaller sizes, from 14 down, it is not necessary to use floss at all, but merely to wrap the tying silk around the shank. In all patterns, the tying silk should be the same color as that of the body, except the Iron Blue Dun which requires the red. Fly heads should be small and neat, permitting the fly quick entry into the stream.

From my experience, the best hooks for these flies are the medium to light wire sproat or limerick styles with tapered eye, short bend and small barb. Such a hook was the Allcock WS210 TDE, Best Hollow Point sproat hooks, which are the ones used in this work. A few years ago, I was able to buy several hundred of these hooks, but I have not seen them available anywhere since then. I have since learned that the hooks were Allcock's second grade in that style and that they offered an even better grade! The best hooks for these flies available today come from England, and the name of the supplier is listed later.

You will have noted that there are two partridge hackle colors, the gray and the brown. When you order these from various material supply houses, you may receive them mixed or separate. The colors chosen for the patterns in this book are my own preference, but in actual use, I don't think it makes much difference, because the color difference is very slight.

For those who have not done any fly tying, I will list some reliable, quick responding sources for tying equipment and supplies.

Buz's, 805 W. Tulare Avenue, Visalia, California 93277

E. Hille, 815 Railway Street, P. O. Box 269, Williamsport, Pa. 17701

Fireside Angler, P. O. Box 823, Melville, N. Y. 11746

Rangeley Region Sports Shop, 28 Main Street, Rangeley, Maine 04970

E. Veniard Ltd., Paramount Warehouses, 138 Northwood Road, Thornton Heath, England CR4 SYG.

This last company sells the finest hooks available today for the flies in this book. Veniard also handles Pearsall's Gossamer Tying Silks in every color imaginable, as well as matching silk flosses, and it is the only company I know that offers liquid wax. The firm also sells an already-mixed pink fur dubbing for the Tups.

The most difficult part in tying any of these soft-hackled flies is the handling, or winding, of the hackle itself. It is soft, small and fragile, and requires the use of rubber tipped hackle-pliers. Even after making hundreds and hundreds of these flies, I still occasionally break off the hackle in the act of winding and have to start with a fresh one. In all ensuing tying instruction, the winding direction is away from the tier. "Back" means toward the bend of the hook. "Forward" means toward the eye.

1. MOUNTING THE TYING THREAD. Fasten a hook in the vise and cover the point of the hook with the jaws so the tying thread will not catch it. Hold one end of the thread in your left hand below the level of the shank with the rest of the thread extending above to your right hand at a 45° angle from bottom left to top right. (*Figure A*) Press the thread against the shank and wind, with your right hand, back over the thread in your left. Three or four turns should be enough to secure the thread. Cut off the short end and let the thread hang by itself on the bobbin.

2. TYING IN AND WINDING THE SILK FLOSS. Use thin floss, or separate heavier floss with a needle or point. The floss should be about four inches long. Hold the end of the floss between thumb and forefinger of the left hand, and set it on top of the hook shank. (*Figure B*) Wind the thread up and then down between thumb and forefinger. Now, pull the thread down on the back side of the hook over the floss and repeat the operation three or four times. (*Figure C*) When done properly, you will feel the tying thread moving down between your fingertips. You can now remove the thumb and forefinger and begin to wind the thread forward toward the eye of the hook. Stop winding about 1/8 of an inch from the eye. (*Figure D*) Wind the floss toward the front of the hook, using your right hand to carry the floss over the top, and your left hand to bring it around the bottom. Catch the end of the floss at the same

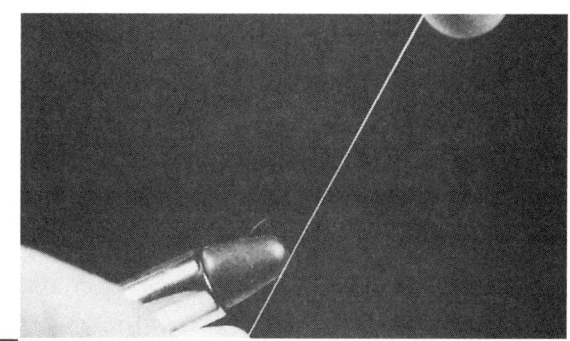

Figure A

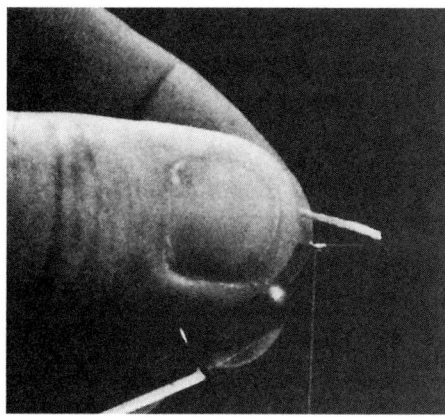

Figure B

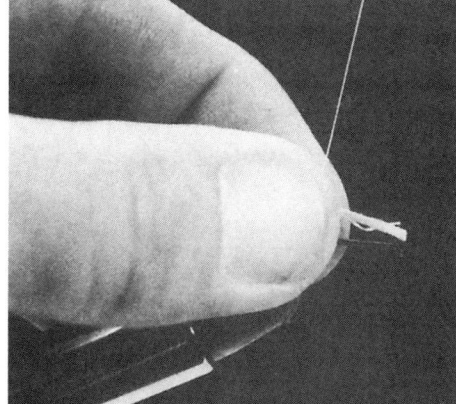

Figure C

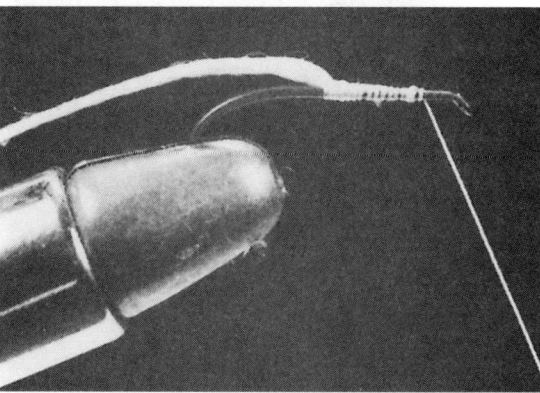

Figure D

place alternately with your left and right hand, so as not to soil it. You should end up winding with the floss in your left hand. Wind the tying thread back toward the floss to catch it with two turns of the thread. Now change hands. Pass the floss to your right hand and the thread to your left. Change hands again. Wind the thread two or three times behind the floss and let the thread hang on its bobbin. Cut the excess floss flush to the hook shank by pressing scissor blades flat against the shank. Wind the thread forward leaving at least 1/16th of an inch bare.

3. PREPARING THE HACKLE. (*Figure E*) The various small bird hackles used are plucked from the skin with the soft down or fuzz still attached to the stem. This material must be stripped off which can be easily done by holding the feather in the thumb and forefinger of the left hand and stripping the down with the same fingers of the right hand, first on one side and then the other. (*Figure F*) Now move your fingers on the feather right towards the tip of it and pull the barbs of the hackle down away from the others so they stand out at right angles from the stem. (*Figure G*)

4. TYING IN THE HACKLE. Hold the bare stem of the hackle at a 45° angle against the side of the hook, with the natural curve of the feather towards the back. Wind the thread around the stem three or four times to secure it firmly to the hook shank, winding towards the front. (*Figure H*) Cut off the excess hackle stem.

5. WINDING THE HACKLE. Grab the tip of the hackle with the rubber tipped hackle pliers. Try to get as many of the end barbs in the jaws as you can, together with the center stem. Pull the hackle upright with the pliers so it is perpendicular to the hook. (*Figure I*) This is rather delicate because the barbs may break or pull out of the jaws as you

Figure E

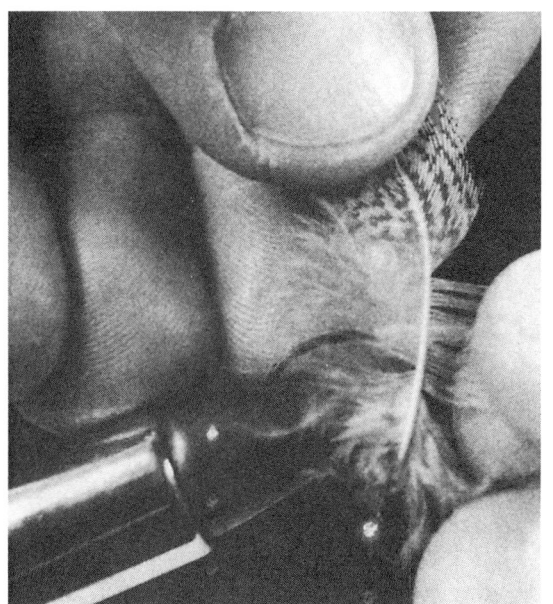

Figure F

Figure H

Figure G

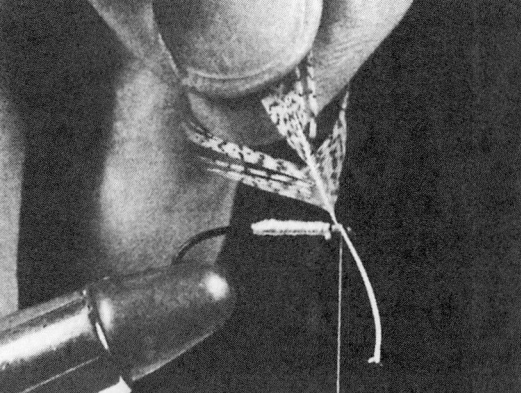

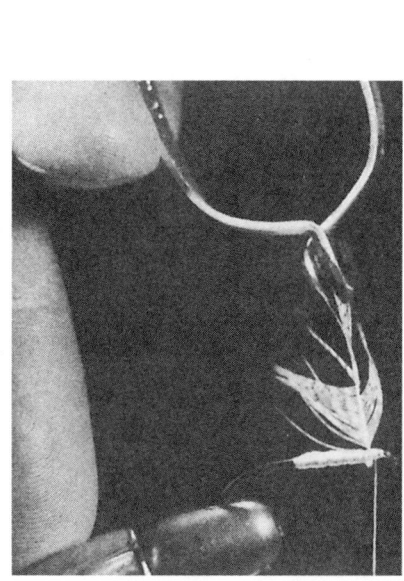

Figure I

apply tension. If they pull out, grab them again with the plier jaws lower down on the stem of the hackle. Now start to wind the hackle around the hook shank. Keep the pliers even as you go around so the hackle will wind on its axis. The hackle barbs will want to stick together, so as you wind with your right hand, separate the barbs with the other to spring them out. Go around one and one half times, or twice, but make sure the pliers are in a down position when you finish. (*Figure J*) Pull the pliers and the remainder of the hackle towards the back and wind the tying thread back through the hackle making sure to catch the stem hanging in the pliers. (*Figure K*) Now wind the thread forward and let it hang on its bobbin. Reach in under the hook with the scissors and cut off the hackle stem. (*Figure L*)

    6. FINISHING THE HEAD. The best finish for any kind of fly is the whip finish. Professionals use it and so do advanced amateurs. It is neat, fast, and fool-proof, and doesn't require head cement. It is difficult to explain and just as hard to show in art work or photos. If you will place your fingers in the same positions as in the photos, chances are you will learn it. Pick up the thread in your left hand about eight inches from the hook and lift the thread so it is on the same plane as the vise. (*Figure M*) Keep the thread taut in your left hand throughout the remaining steps. Place the two first fingers of your right hand in back of and over the thread, with the palm down. (*Figure N*) Now twist the two fingers forward, spreading them apart slightly. You should have turned your hand over so now the palm is up. Now you have half a knot between your right hand and your left. Pull with your left hand and follow the tension until the half knot is pulled against the head of the

Figure J

Figure K

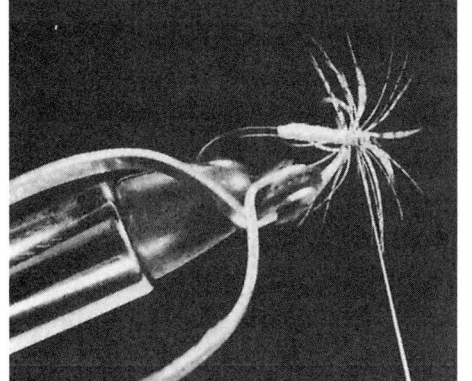

Figure L

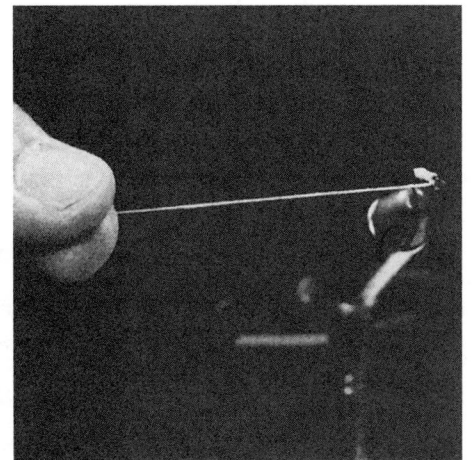

Figure M

Figure N

hook, but keeping the right hand two fingers spread apart. (*Figure O*) The thread in your right hand should be across the middle of the first joint of your forefinger and right in the crease of the first joint of your second finger, both of which will be behind the hook. (*Figure P*) Move the second finger up under the first one, keeping the thread tight over the middle of the first joint and wind the thread around the back side of the hook. As you do this, you will feel the tension shift from your forefinger to the second finger. (*Figure Q*) Come around until your fingers are in the same position as when you first twisted them over. Before you go around the second time, pull the second finger back away from the forefinger so you will feel the thread again right in the crease of the first joint. Go around three or four times in the same manner and stop at the top of the last turn. Your fingers will again be behind the hook. Place the third finger of your right hand against the thread on the back side of the hook. (*Figure R*) Pull the thread with your left hand and you will feel the knot tighten around your first two fingers. Tilt the two fingers toward you, taking pressure off the second finger. Pull it back out of the knot and catch the loop in your thumb and forefinger. Continue to pull the thread with your left hand and guide the loop downward toward the tip of the head, keeping the third finger against the knot on the back. (*Figure S*) Now cut the thread close up under the head.

The foregoing steps are for use in making any of the floss and hackle flies mentioned in this book. You might want to experiment with different short, soft hackles from other birds in your area such as bobwhite or quail, doves, waterfowl and pheasant, although most of the hackles on the latter birds are too large.

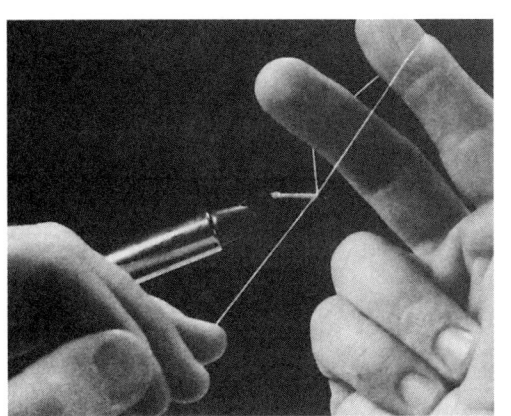

Figure P

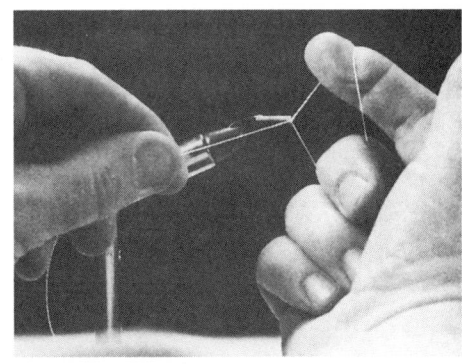

Figure O

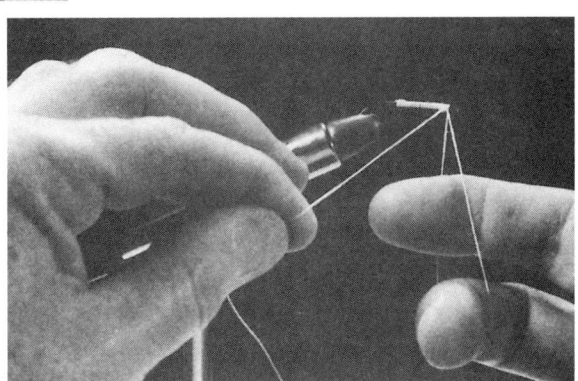

Figure Q

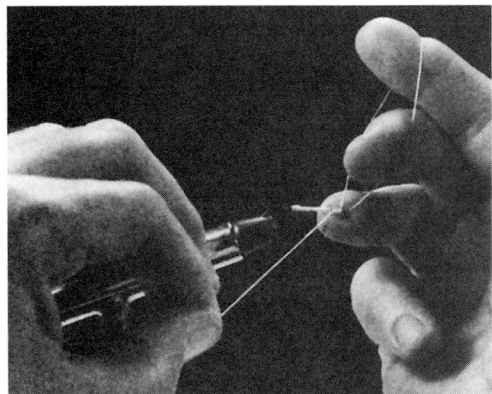

Figure R

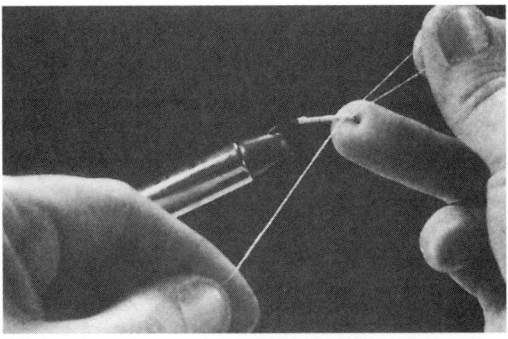

Figure S

Flies such as the Tups Indispensable, with fur thorax, call for the extra step of spinning the fur on the tying thread and winding it in before you bind on the hackles.

There are many ways to spin fur on thread. The easiest method, I think, is to do it while the tying thread is hanging on its bobbin. This would be done at the end of step two, after you have wound the floss just two thirds of the way up the shank. You will need liquid wax and a hare's face.

Coat two inches of the thread with liquid wax by dipping a bodkin into the wax and applying it to the thread. Cut off some fur with the scissor blades held flat against the skin. (*Figure T*) Lift the scissors with the fur on the blades and dump the fur on your thigh or on the fly tying table. (*Figure U*) The hunk of fur should be about 1/2 an inch across and about 3/4 of an inch long. Lift the fur gingerly, with your thumb and forefinger, and place it right against the waxed tying thread. It will stick there. (*Figure V*) Now with your thumb and forefinger pinch the fur and tying thread together and roll them between your fingers. (*Figure W*) Wind the thread and fur around the hook towards the front. The fur thorax should not be more than 1/8 of an inch wide even on a size 10 hook. (*Figure X*) If there is not enough fur, recoat more tying thread and add more. If there is too much, pinch the thread and fur with your thumbnail and strip it right down off the thread. Now complete the fly with the hackle and the whip finish.

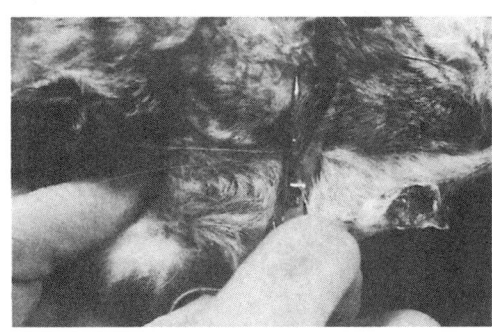

Figure T

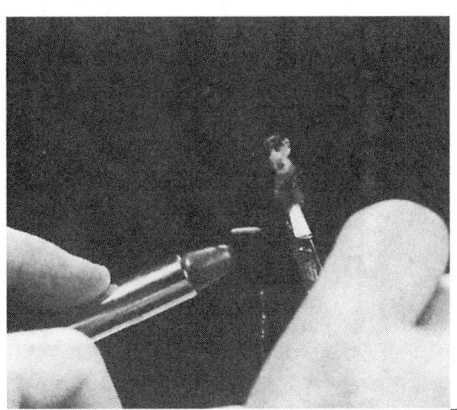

Figure U

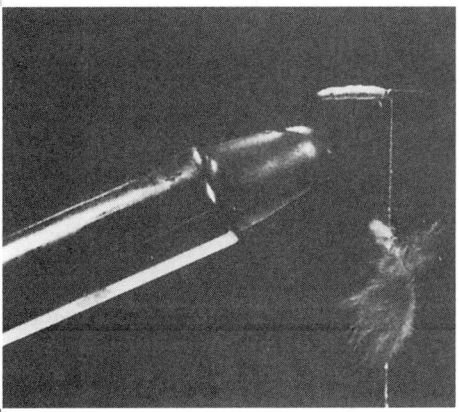

Figure V

Figure W

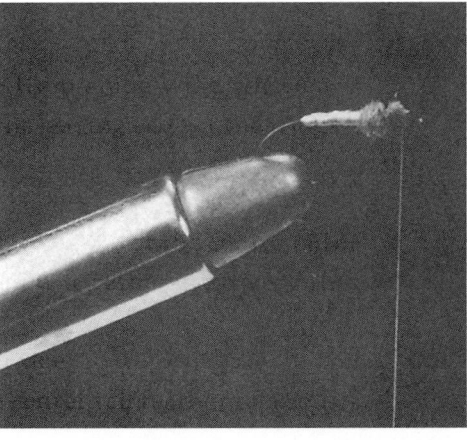

Figure X

Chapter VIII

Soft-hackled flies are fished best in the kind of water most fly fishermen like best. It is the kind of water with sufficient current speed to move the line rapidly downstream. It is also the kind of water which will quickly whisk away a loose fly should it accidently fall into the river from your fly box. The swiftness of the water in this sort of stream is not so great, however, that wading downstream is difficult. Sufficient pressure from the current nudging you along makes it seem natural to be going downstream instead of up.

The right river for the soft-hackled fly will be more rough surfaced than smooth which means, of course, that the water is running over rocks and stones, sunken logs or stumps and weed beds. It is a good sign if here and there one can see an occasional outcropping either above or just below the surface.

The rough textured surface also means that the depth is not too great. The soft-hackle is not at its best in more than four feet of water; in fact a shallower stream is better, because the fly rarely sinks more than three or four inches.

Productive water for the soft-hackled fly is fairly straight and riffly, with long, gentle bends and little variance in depth from one side to the other. This is not normally the most scenic of trout rivers, in fact to the non-fisher, this kind of water looks much too shallow. "There wouldn't be any fish in there," they say. I find much of this kind of water ignored also by many practising fly fishermen, who seem to prefer deeper pools with shallow water on one side. Wading is relatively easy under these conditions and it is true the fish do tend to "hole up" in this kind of water. But so do the fishermen.

There are two such pools or runs called Barn Hole Number 1 and Barn Hole Number 2 on the Madison River, just inside the west entrance to Yellowstone Park. They are very popular, because they are easily fished and they are close to West Yellowstone. Frequently, each pool is occupied by two, three, or four fishermen. However, there is a very, fast, choppy riffle just above Number 1, which hardly anyone ever fishes. Across this water is strung a cable on which Park Rangers traverse the river in some sort of spring-released or gravity driven chair. I like to start in above that cable and work down. The current here is very fast; one can't wade it much over the knees. There is no time for mending, but it really isn't needed. The surface is broken by a number of boulders and a good many big fish lie there.

On this stretch, I seldom fail to take a fish up to 15 inches with one of the soft-hackles, preferably a Tups or one of the other thorax patterns. I have missed some rises in there that really jarred me.

One such fish, encountered in October of 1973, must have been in the seven or eight pound class. In October, when big browns and rainbow migrate up the Madison from Hebgen Lake, fish of that size can surely be found in this river. At that time I was situated below the cable using a size 12 Pheasant Tail. I had worked down the stretch without finding any interest from a fish, when I had a powerful nip at the fly, but no real take. Whenever this happens, it is wise not to move another step and not to change the casting length of the line. You may have put the fish down with the pricking or touching of the fly, but the second chance at an eager fish is worth the cast. My second cast was identical. The big fish came again and this time was hooked firmly. As with many steelhead I have caught on the fly, this one charged diagonally towards the opposite bank and downstream pulling line off the reel at incredible speed. My God! This can't be! Not on a size 12 soft-hackle. But true enough—it was all over in a flash. I reeled up looking anxiously for the broken line, leader or fly. I had the line. I had the leader. And I had the fly. I was puzzled until I checked the hook closely. The very tip of the barb was gone, broken as easily as a spider's web by that big fish.

An angling experience of this sort raises some interesting questions about what a fish, particularly a big fish, will eat or what it can see. Why will it attack such an obviously small insect or artificial when it would require several hundred of them to make even a small appetizer? How much energy must it spend to rise or move to one side or the other after the tiny prey? Is there so much protein, so many nutrients and calories in a small insect that just one or a couple will sustain a large fish for a long period of time? How does the fish see such tiny artificials or real insects zipping by it at high speed in broken water?

A.H.E. Wood said there was very little a salmon didn't see, and we can assume the trout sees just as much. Without answers to all these questions, we can only marvel at what remarkable creatures trout really are. Perhaps our inability to know all there is to know about them provides the mystery that makes their pursuit so fascinating and delightful.

Number 1. Barn Hole on the Madison is just below the fast riffly stretch I have mentioned. It is ideal for the soft-hackle, and at its best during the months of September and October. On the evening of the same day I lost the big fish, I landed and released two browns and a rainbow, all between eighteen and twenty inches, during forty-five minutes of the finest and most exciting fishing I have ever had in my life. It all happened from 6:45 to 7:30. After releasing the first fish, the Partridge and Green soft-hackle resembled hardly anything at all, but it was then too dark to change. After the second fish, the floss was torn to shreds with just a couple of barbs of the partridge hackle still hanging on. After the third fish, the hook was practically bare, yet I think I could have taken still another had not total darkness and the evening chill settled on the river.

Most fishermen on the Barnhole Number 1, never fish enough of it. They start in at the top, wade down a hundred feet or so and stop where the pool levels off into a 300 foot long broad shallow tail. Three years ago in that tail, I got my first sixteen inch brown from the Madison

Barn Hole No. 2 on the Madison River in Yellowstone National Park. A very fine run for soft-hackled flies.

with a soft-hackle, where the water was barely more than a foot deep. Half a dozen fishermen in and out of the water above me looked on in amazement.

The kind of water least suitable for the soft-hackled fly is the multi-bend river with deep, black pools, short, abrupt tails and fast lips. Pocket water like the Roaring Fork in Aspen, even though it carries a large stock of trout, is not entirely appropriate for the soft-hackle. Yet, the sister stream of the Roaring Fork, the Frying Pan River, yields very well to the soft-hackles. Similarly, the East River of the Gunnison responds to the soft-hackles, but its more tumultuous, pockety, hard to wade cousin, Taylor Fork, gives up its trout reluctantly to the same fly.

Many of the broad riffly stretches of the Madison, both in the Park and out of it, and the Gallatin, especially midway between West Yellowstone and Bozeman, are beautiful rivers for these flies.

In Michigan, the ten mile long, no-closed season, fly-only stretch of the Pere Marquette is productive all year long. During the spring of 1972, on April 10, with snow still in the woods, and temperatures at, or just above, freez-

OPPOSITE: *Selection of the author's favorite soft-hackled flies.* Top row: *Partridge-and-Yellow (with fur thorax); Partridge-and-Orange (with fur thorax); Snipe-and-Yellow.* Second row: *Snipe-and-Purple; March Brown Spider; Partridge-and-Yellow.* Third row: *Starling-and-Herl; Pheasant Tail; Grouse-and-Orange; Partridge-and-Green (with fur thorax).* Bottom row: *Partridge-and-Green; Partridge-and-Orange; Iron Blue Dun; and Tups Indispensable. Photo by the author.*

Soft-hackled fly in special flow-tank to demonstrate action of the long, loose hackles. This photo shows fly with no drag.

ABOVE: *Same fly with current (or fly motion) activating hackles.*

BELOW: *Same fly with full action of water, moving hackle back into streamlined position. Nemes recommends natural action of current to activate hackles rather than heavy jerking by angler. Photos by the author.*

ing, I took two small browns on soft-hackles, while fishing with larger flies, before and after, for steelhead.

There is some nice, riffly water on the Muskegon above Newaygo where good-sized rainbows take the soft-hackle very well. On the Au Sable system in Michigan, stretches of the North Branch (where I first used the partridge hackles) yield well, while the South Branch seems too sluggish, sandy, and siltish. The main branch has plentiful soft-hackle water, especially in the lower stretches, but heavy canoe traffic on weekends prevents much fishing from being done.

Further north, the Boardman, although beautiful and yielding of big browns at night, has never been a good soft-hackle river.

The best and most productive stretch I ever found for these flies is on the Firehole in Yellowstone Park. The water I speak of is above the canyon, but not as far up as the hot steam geysers. Here the river is quite broad and flat. The bottom is of mixed gravel and rock with heavy weed beds rising and bending out of sand knolls. The current is steady, with a broken surface. In this water, rainbows respond to the flies better than do the browns. When I asked Pat Barnes, tackle shop proprietor and guide in West Yellowstone, why this was, he said the browns were on the bottom while the rainbows ranged higher in the stream, accounting for the larger number of them caught on the shallow-riding soft-hackled flies.

The soft-hackled fly on this water in August, September, and even October, is an amazing performer in these days of controlled and crowded streams generally stocked short of the demand. The Firehole, however, seems filled to the brim with wild rainbow and brown, and what must be tremendous, subaqueous insect life for the soft-hackles to work so well.

Schwiebert and Charles E. Brooks, (*The Trout and the Stream*, 1974), both say a good proportion of this underwater life consists of the caddis fly pupae.

Fish in the Firehole are often seen tailing or bulging, an encouraging sign on any water for these flies. True, I have never taken a sixteen inch fish on the Firehole, which is now the minimum legal taking-size on this river and the Madison, but my average day's take does not fall far short of W.C. Stewart, who said, "And he is not worthy of the name of angler who cannot, in any day of the month, when the water is clear, kill from fifteen to twenty pounds weight of trout in any county in the south of Scotland."

The Firehole trout are fat with small heads, and average thirteen or fourteen inches in length. The soft-hackle will take twenty-five to forty of these per day, and though I have never weighed them, or kept any, their total weight must be more than Stewart's figure.

Though the Firehole is good to me and to my soft-hackles, it is not the same for other fishermen I have met there using either dry flies, western streamers, or other kinds of wet flies or nymphs. Many fishermen I have talked with said they had very few fish. Perhaps it is because the productive part of the water I'm speaking of is largely overlooked. It runs right along the main road to Old Faithful, and if the angler is not too far in the water, he will have to watch his back cast for fear of catching a tourist's car.

One minor accomplishment with the soft-hackled fly occurred here five years ago, during the early part of October. I was winding up a phenomenal day's fishing. I hooked and released at least forty trout, mostly rainbow, on the Orange and Partridge and the Yellow and Partridge. The rises missed numbered into the fifties. I was sated and it was getting dark, but I was still going.

Chuck Fothergill drove up in his VW bus and pulled over to the side to see how I was doing. We had met a couple of years earlier on the Madison in the Park, and then later at his tackle shop in Aspen. It was he who introduced me to his beloved Roaring Fork and showed me how he takes thirty or forty trout per day, fishing upstream with weighted nymphs and weighted leader. Our styles were at complete opposites. He was on the bottom. I was on the top. He used lead. I used nothing but the bare fly. He fished upstream. I fished down.

Sticking to my own style and fly, he could outfish me five to one on the Roaring Fork, and I was amazed and a little stunned by his ability. He once said he never saw anyone fish the nymph downstream with a slack line and without any weight as I did. And I think the soft-hackles were new to him.

When he stopped on the Firehole to watch me, I was elated. I told him I had caught more trout that day than I could count. Would he watch me while I tried to take another? Yes, okay. Oh, that I could just catch one more and do it as quickly and easily as I had with all the others. I stepped into the water and cast. Not a long cast, and the mend was not required. In the classic way, with no drag, almost as though rehearsed by the trout, the fly, and me, a fourteen or fifteen inch rainbow acted the part beautifully. I looked up at Chuck, the fish doing his thing to the end.

Chuck said, "Okay, you convinced me."

Chapter IX

If one were fishing dry fly and decided instantly to switch to any of the soft-hackle flies and the mending method I've described, he wouldn't have to change a thing except the fly itself. His dry fly rod would be from seven to eight and one-half feet long. His line would be a floater. And the leader would be tapered to a pretty fine point, say two, three, or at the most, four pounds.

The rod may be fiberglass or bamboo, the leader knotted or knotless, and the line probably one of the new, plastic floating lines.

He would have to change styles, however, from upstream to across and down, and bring in the occasional mend mentioned earlier.

I still use bamboo, possibly because my fishing life started and grew with this material, and I have returned to silk lines during the last couple of years. I guess the reason for preferring the bamboo and the silk lines are the same. Both are solid with no air space in the center as is the case with the new plastic fly lines.

The air space puts me off. In a glass rod, it makes the butt too large and the tip too obvious. The rod feels "light as a feather," but seems to lack stamina in the middle.

In a plastic line, the trapped-in air cells inflate the diameter of the line at least a size or two larger than the same size or weight line in silk.

The larger diameter of the plastic line causes more wind resistance and cannot be controlled in casting or mending as easily as the silk line. With any amount of backing, the plastic line also needs a larger capacity reel, because of the extra bulk.

It is true, the silk line has to be greased and greased regularly to float. But as one British writer said recently, one can play tunes on the silk line by greasing only a part of it, leaving the last few feet ungreased, giving the angler a sinking tip. Or, one can leave the whole line ungreased, in which case all of it will sink.

New silk lines manufactured in England by King Eider are now made with a silicone dressing which is supposed not to require drying the line. I usually uncoil the line at night on a sofa, and grease it in the morning before going out. The line will require another greasing at midday in order to keep it floating. String it up between two trees or lay it on the grass or weeds—let it dry for a few minutes and regrease.

There are no special qualifications for the leader in this style of fishing. My leaders are never much longer than the rod I'm using. I make them up from Maxima leader material, starting at the butt with a number 6 line at 20 pounds, then 15, 12, 10, 8, 6, 4 and 3 depending on how small a fly I'm fishing. Each succeeding piece of material is slightly longer than the preceding. With an eight foot rod and a number 7 line, I start with 25 pound material at the butt.

Maxima is the finest material I have ever used for leaders. It seems to have the right stiffness to roll out high on the back cast and to turn over the fly on the forward cast. Even though there are other monofilaments with smaller given diameters, I like it better because of the color (or lack of it) and the transparency which makes it difficult to see in the water. Dry or wet, it has the feel of the silkworm gut leaders we used many years ago. The material also ties and holds the blood knot very well. I have never seen leaders ready-made from this material, so the angler will have to buy it on spools and make his own.

When Pritt and Stewart were taking their fifteen and twenty pounds of trout per day with the soft-hackle flies, they were doing it with more than one fly on the cast. In fact, Stewart says, "The number of flies that should be used at a time is a matter upon which great diversity of opinion exists; some anglers never use more than three, while others occasionally use a dozen." He goes on to say the bigger the water, the more flies the angler might use.

Today, when the fly is taking very well, it is tempting to put a second or even third fly on the leader, in the hopes of catching two trout at a time. I have done this quite a few times, and there was a time when I was using two and three flies quite often.

It can be a good practice to start out fishing this way, provided that more than one fly is permitted on the water,

The author mending a soft-hackle down the Mettowee near Dorset, Vermont.

and one does not know what kind of subaqueous life exists there, or what artificial is taking. Eventually it is possible to switch to the single, most successful fly, after it has proved itself over the others. That a particular fly appeals to the trout more than the others, even in the soft-hackles, happens quite frequently at which point it is really quite useless to have the others on.

The best way to attach the second or third fly to the leader is to use one of the blood knot ends of the leader material. Instead of cutting this end after the knot is tied, just let it hang out six or seven inches and tie the dropper fly to it. This should be done toward the fine, tip end of the leader where the material is fine enough to let the fly work.

It is, however, more sporting and, I feel, more in the classic tradition to use only one fly. Besides, the dropper or droppers will invariably catch each other or the tail fly during the act of casting and create knots other than those tied in on purpose. In weedy rivers, moreover, the junction of the dropper has a habit of collecting floating vegetation which has to be removed from time to time.

Chapter X

If one is not an absolute grouch, he will invariably meet other fishermen along the trout stream who, from strangers, will turn into friends. Nonetheless, there is a natural inclination to keep to one's self, especially since the sport demands the singular concentration of the caster. There is also a tendency towards natural selfishness in keeping the location of the good pools and riffles to one's self and not divulging the fly pattern one knows is good on that particular water.

I have met a few fishermen who wouldn't give me the time of day, let alone a valuable tip which might help me take a fish. But I have met many more who would share with me, a perfect stranger, his flies, leaders, and his most productive water.

Such a man is Jim Rader. Jim lives in Baldwin, Michigan, just a few miles from the Pere Marquette. His home is modest. His job is running machinery for the state conservation department. As a native, or "local" he does everything which can be done in the state of Michigan in the way of fishing and hunting. He starts the fishing season (he really never ends it) going after steelhead in March on the Pere Marquette, now open to fly-fishing-only all year long, from Route 37, downstream for about ten miles.

On the Pere Marquette, the Little Manistee, and other steelhead-bearing rivers nearby, he will take seventy or eighty steelhead in a year, many on flies and many on spinners of his own making. He was one of the first fishermen in the area to take giant Chinook, close to forty pounds, as they came up the rivers to spawn. He also fishes from a boat in Lake Michigan for lake trout, now making a comeback in that water. And he is one of the best trout fly fishermen I have ever met.

His knowledge of fly fishing is staggering, yet I doubt if he has ever read a book on the subject. He casts tiny dry flies, big "caddis" at night, and weighted steelhead flies, all with equal ease and proficiency, yet he doesn't own an Orvis, Leonard, Thomas, or Young. He knows when the brown drake, the iron blue, or the "caddis" will come off and when to be on this river or that river, yet I have never heard him use words such as "entomology," "pupae," "ephemera," and the like.

He frequently takes browns to seven pounds on flies, and fish of twenty inches are commonplace to him.

I met Jim, without introduction, in Ed's Tackle and Fly Shop in Baldwin. He was there to buy flies for some evening fishing while I was checking hatches with the proprietor, and buying insect repellent.

Jim is a straight-forward and unpretentious man. After

Doug Vanerka on the Little Manistee using a soft-hackled fly in late April.

the usual fishermen's salutations, he asked me directly if I wanted to go fishing with him that evening.

An offer like that from a "local" is worth more than gold and if you ever get one, don't turn it down. Even though I was a nonresident, I was quite familiar with the P.M. I knew many of the access roads; knowledge which is absolutely necessary to fly fishermen in any trout area. And I had been fishing the river since 1948.

I followed Jim to his home and we transferred rods, waders and other gear into his "fishing car," a 1957 Chevy.

As we drove in a downstream direction toward Bowman's Bridge, Jim was talking about the "caddis." They were not up yet in full force, but were to be seen several miles downstream working their way up slowly. A couple of nights before, however, Jim had seen a big fish working on a stretch of the river above the bridge.

Like other "local" fly fishermen, Jim was a trophy trout hunter. All of them were in perpetual pursuit of the biggest fish in the county. Their competition with each other carried with it no prizes. The reward would be the simple remark from any or all of them, over beers in the local tap, that Jim or Fred or Al was a goddamn good fisherman. In this "club," the big fish of Michigan are hunted by the locals just as bighorn sheep and royal elk are hunted in Montana and Idaho.

For every night of fishing, the locals spend at least another evening or two just walking the bank, rodless and waderless. They listen and watch . . . walk and listen and watch some more. This is no easy chore, for there are no pathways along these silent, secret stretches of the river. These hunters cross mud-filled spring bogs, and crawl through jungles of weed and shrub, often in total darkness.

Invariably they find the trophy, for these huge trout are not silent feeders, but loud and clamorous with spectacular bravery.

Once the fish shows himself to one of these dogged pursuers, he is doomed. The fisherman marks the spot, studies the water, the casting positions and angles (if it is not pitch black), where to enter the river, where to cross it and where to get out. The hunter then backs away and thinks about that fish for a day or two before coming back and taking him.

Jim and I crossed Bowman's Bridge and turned upstream off the main road. In all my years of fishing the river, I had never seen that track before. It was so obscure, I don't think I could find it again by myself.

We drove in, the old Chevy grinding through the sand with tree branches scraping the sides of the car. When we came to a little clearing and parked, the river was not far away.

This was moderately big water running over an all-sand bottom. The current was strong with a fairly even surface. There were deep, dark pools which created difficulties in crossing the stream. Trees, tag alders, and stumps lined both sides of the river. It was spooky, but it was the kind of water which one felt harbored big browns.

There was still a lot of light left in the sky, and even though the "caddis" were not expected yet, we started fishing right away.

Jim put me in exactly where he had seen the big fish a couple of nights before and pointed out where the rise had been. I worked the spot with big "caddis" patterns and then with a Green Drake bucktail, but I couldn't find the trout.

Jim was downstream. I decided to work down to him and switched to a Partridge and Green. As I started wading down, I was casting the soft-hackle against the far side of the stream, under the bank. A light colored fly on the water against the bank attracted a nice brown which took it with a little commotion.

Was this the big fish Jim had seen higher up in the stream? I changed to the Partridge and Yellow and cast it two feet ahead of the rise and the fish took it just as it had the natural a moment before. It was a good fish, but not of the gigantic proportions described by Jim.

As I played him, Jim hurried up. I landed the sixteen inch brown just as Jim got there and was taking the partridge hackle out of the fish's mouth. The fly was a size 12 with the hackle all matted down against the hook. Jim saw the fly and asked what it was. He claimed he had never seen one like it before. When I showed him my fly box, filled with nothing but the soft-hackles, he was a little amazed.

I gave him four or five to try and he went off downstream. I returned to fishing, too, but I could hear Jim yell everytime he had a rise on his new flies.

Later that evening, in Jim's kitchen, I tied a dozen mixed soft-hackles for him. Since I was leaving the next morning, I knew I wouldn't see him for a while. In the meanwhile I knew that the flies would have a good and convincing tryout.

In August, I received the following letter from Jim:

Dear Syl:

I'm sending you some partridge feathers I picked up and skinned out. One old hen and two young ones, and will save you more when I get some. I still haven't been able to get any wood duck feathers but will keep trying.

You made a believer out of me with your nymphs [*soft-hackles*]. I finally took two nice 20 inch browns on them, but I wore them out and would like to get some more if you have them.

By now, you probably have heard that the fly-only water won the fight and will be open year around, so you will be able to do some spring fly fishing. [*A reference to the Michigan Department of Natural Resources' decision to restrict the Pere Marquette to fly only*]. I did pretty good on the fly hatches. I took sixty-four, the biggest seven pounds. Now, I'm working on the lake trout out in Lake Michigan and doing real good.

Sincerely,
JIM RADER

Chapter XI

A minor revolution has been taking place during the last few years in the style of fly fishing for steelhead as practiced in the west. The style has been turned topsy-turvy from big, heavy-weight flies, sinking shooting heads; to small, sparsely dressed, unweighted flies, and the floating or greased line.

Before, where a steelhead fisherman would use 2's and 4's, he's now using 6's, 8's, and even 10's. Instead of raking the bottom as before, his fly is now riding in the upper four inches of the stream. Where he used to let the line belly in the current, he is now mending the floating line just as A.H.E. Wood did when he caught all those salmon in Scotland during the earlier part of this century.

The ghost of Wood haunts the banks of the Clearwater, Snake, and Salmon Rivers in Idaho; the Grande Ronde, Imnaha, and Deschutes Rivers in Oregon; and the Rouge,

Umpqua, and Klamath Rivers in California. Here, mending fly fishermen are now having fun they never dreamed of. Steelhead to twenty pounds, committing head and tail rises like small trout, are now taken with this new technique likened by some to dry fly fishing. The thrill matches the one to be had when fishing Atlantic salmon with the fly, without the high price tag generally associated with it. In the west, all the angler needs is the fishing license, the equipment, and the method.

Except for the smaller rods, lighter lines, and, of course, smaller, soft-hackled flies that method is the same one I use for trout. Once the angler learns the system for trout, he can, with the addition of the double haul, step right into any of the great riffles on these rivers and try for the fishing thrill of his lifetime.

In Chapter IV, I briefly described Wood's greased line mending method as discussed in Jock Scott's book. Now we can go in and out of the book, and get answers to special problems right from the horse's mouth.

QUESTION? What's the theory of greased line fishing?

ANSWER: *"The basic idea is to use the line as a float for, and controlling agent of, the fly; to suspend the fly just beneath the surface of the water, and to control its path in such a way that it swims diagonally down and across the stream, entirely free from the slightest pull on the line."*

QUESTION? How does one know when the fly is dragging if he can't see the fly?

ANSWER: *"Watch the line for bellying, or whenever you feel the pull of the rod, you know that drag has been set up."*

QUESTION? How does one mend with the line lying on the water?

ANSWER: *"The line should be removed from the surface of the water by raising the rod almost horizontally and keeping the arm stiff."* (I said earlier that I held the rod parallel to the water, but as high as I could off the water. I still think this is the best way with the single-handed short rods we use for trout fishing today. A.H.E. Wood mixed his salmon fishing with a single-handed rod of 12 feet and longer, two-handed rods up to 14 feet long. The longer rod will help in mending, however.)

QUESTION? What's wrong with drag?

ANSWER: *"As there is little a fish does not see, the fly ought to behave naturally all the time, as an insect or other live creature would do in the water, and try to let the fly move with all the eddies it meets, as will any living thing that is trying to move in the water with the stream and across."*

QUESTION? What is "leading"?

ANSWER: *"By moving the rod in advance of the line—but not of course dragging it—you help the fly to swim more downstream than across."*

QUESTION? How will I know when I'm doing it right?

ANSWER: *"The greased line, if fished properly (and this is by no means the case every time) has no drag and often is all slack and crooked."*

The last answer brings to mind the classic photograph of the expert dry fly fisherman, having just cast his line in loose "S" curves.

A very nice riffle for the soft-hackled fly on the Hoback River, south of Jackson Hole Wyoming. The deep side, up to three feet, is on the right. This and similar riffles should be fished from the shallow side, the angler starting in the fast water at the top of the riffle. Cutthroats on this stretch of the river respond with enthusiasm to the soft-hackled fly.

A question must come to the mind of the reader, as it did to mine when I first started reading about the greased line. What to do when the line eventually swings clear around to the fisherman's side as it must do in any kind of current?

The answer is—nothing, because it's time to recast. The lower part of the cast in greased-line fishing with the soft-hackles is the least important. Lawrie said Scottish and border fishermen never even let their spiders or other soft-hackles go that far, but that they were fishing just the upper part of the cast, without drag, casting short and frequently.

Greased Line Fishing for Salmon, by Jock Scott, is one of the finest books on fly fishing instruction I have ever read. Even if you never fish for salmon, or get a chance to try the system for steelhead, the lessons contained in it will serve you well in the fishing of the soft-hackles, or other kinds of nymphs and wet flies.

Two other books, *Salmon Fishing,* Frederick Hill (1948), and *The Floating Line for Salmon and Sea-Trout,* Anthony Crossley (1939), also offer insight on the floating, mended line.

Chapter XII

There is a little, light mark more than half-way up the butt section of my seven and one-half foot rod which measures just over twenty-two inches from the butt of the reel seat. The mark will be there forever to remind me of my big fish, because I never keep big fish, though I do sometimes keep a small one or two for a camp supper.

I don't believe in mounting fish and even though I am, and have been for many years, an avid duck hunter, I also don't believe in mounting birds, or any other animal, big or small. The memory should be enough, and always has been for me without benefit of some dusty specimen on the wall of the den or the office.

The memory can be pulled out of the mind or heart whenever wanted. I dwell on this particular memory quite often during the quiet, winter months, and will now come as close as I ever will to displaying it as a trophy.

I was photographing big crawler tractors in Idaho and Montana six years ago in the early part of September. I finished my work near Butte on a Friday and drove to Ennis to fish the Madison there on the weekend.

When I saw the river near the town the next morning, I realized why this was a great mecca for the fly fisherman. At Ennis, and below, the Madison splits up into several small streamlets of which I fished a couple, taking a few small specimens.

For a few hours that afternoon I watched the labs. Goldens and a few Chesapeakes perform in a regional retriever trial near town.

I still wanted to try the river upstream and learned about a ranch two miles up where fishermen were permitted to cross the private land to get to the western side of the river.

I liked this part of the Madison much more than the downstream stretch. It was big, strong water with long, thin islands dividing it here and there. You could fish close to the near bank or venture out closer to the islands without getting too far into the treacherous mainstream. The current was powerful with a nice, broken surface, and even on the "lee" side of the islands, wading was difficult.

It was good water for the soft-hackles, and I was having fun with frequent takes from smaller fish.

Fifty yards upstream there were two islands, a very long one on the left, near the center of the stream, and a shorter one on the right. Between them there was a beautiful scour that was sure to be four feet deep. I waded straight up on a line with the smaller island intending to go all the way up and fish the scour down. About half-way up the length of it, still wading and not yet casting, I saw my big fish.

He rose just once, in the middle of the scour, not more than eight or ten feet away from me. The rise was slow and deliberate, head first, with the big, sinuous body curving over for the downward dive. There were no signs of a hatch or single fly on the water. I don't know what he took.

In showing himself to me, at such close range, the fish must have seen me too, and I slacked off back downstream. I was not going to fish him now. I would give him plenty of rest so that he might forget me, if, indeed, he did see me. We could make an appointment for tomorrow night at the same time, I thought.

The next day, I returned to the field trials. Being a large regional event, there were many good dogs and their classy retrieves kept me pre-occupied. At about five I went back to the motel to get the Orvis, the waders, and the flies. In the motel room, I checked and greased the line and tied on a new leader.

It was six by the time I waded out to the edge of the scour. This time I steered a wider course, with a keen eye out for any signs of my friend. I saw none. When I was at the head of the scour, just below the smaller island, I put on a Tups.

I was above the spot where I had seen him—on purpose. I didn't want to undershoot him; I wanted to put the Tups right where he lived.

I cast several times, throwing nice slack line and moving down very slowly. Something welled up inside me. The fly was running down the center of the scour. He had to see it, if he were there.

He did.

The rise was almost the same. He didn't come so far out

of the water as he had 24 hours earlier, but there he was, and I had him.

I looked at my watch. It was 6:05.

What a difference a big fish makes. He moves hardly at all at the beginning. The feeling is of authority. The heaviness is inviolable. You know this is not going to be easy and you feel a little outclassed.

Things started to happen slowly. At first, no big runs, no curving leaps high in the air, just the fish lying there, jerking his head like a dog. When is he going to go, when is he going to realize this could be the fight of his life?

He started upstream taking line off the reel, the handle spinning wildly under my hand. He was going fast and could have kept right on going up around the island and down on the other side and that would have been it. But he turned and came back down and we started to slug it out in the scour.

Now we settled down to a long series of runs up and down and over against the bank of the island. More sulking and holding and jerking of the head. He never relented. I never slacked off. I just wanted to tire him out, to pull him by my feet and see what he looked like close up.

Really, I overplayed him, and I'm sure that a more eager fisherman could have brought him in much sooner. But finally he was at my feet on his side and it was 6:35.

I never took him out of the water, but set the Orvis over him, the butt of the rod at the tip of his tail. I pinched the rod with my thumb and forefinger right over the end of his nose to measure him, and held the place tight so as not to lose it. Then with my left hand, I unhooked the Tups. I turned the big fish over to right him and gave him a little shove upstream and he was gone. I scratched a mark on the rod with my fly scissors where my thumb and forefinger were and started to head for dry land.

A yellow cow dog was on the bank, apparently watching me the whole time. Before I got to the shore, he was in the water swimming out to me, struggling hard against the current. When he was up to me, he turned to follow me out. We got to the shore and started up the bank. I walked slowly across the meadow, the yellow cow dog following and he seemed as happy as I was.

PART TWO

I am happy to introduce the new material for this edition of *The Soft-Hackled Fly* and to include a few words about the use of soft hackles in slightly abbreviated form as tiny soft hackles. Since my book on soft hackles was first published in 1975, fly fishing has changed dramatically. Anglers just can't get enough of it and are now finding ways to extend their season and their happiness fishing in home waters and in faraway waters in faraway places for all kinds of fish.

Midge fishing or fishing with very tiny flies belongs to this quest. It is a relatively new method. Not too long ago, anglers and angling writers used to say you'll never catch trout feeding on those tiny insects. They called them the fisherman's curse and other derogatory names because trout fed on them voraciously. All an angler could do was watch while the fish fed and thumbed their noses at them.

Anglers and angling literature bad-mouthed the tiny insects. They called them smuts and midges and no-see-ums and other less printable words. Still, several good books have been published clearly identifying the insects and giving instructions on how to tie and fish the new tiny fly patterns. An early book on the subject going back to the late 1800s was written by F. M. Halford and deals with not the wet fly but the dry. And some of America's fishing writers like Vince Marinaro recognized the value of minuscule trout insects and wrote well about them. Charles Brooks, who was a good friend of mine, wrote a book on the Henry's Fork that deals, to a certain extent, with minuscule trout insects found on that great trout stream. Others have followed: *Micropatterns: Tying and Fishing the Small Fly* by Darrel Martin, *Small Fly Adventures in the West* by Neale Streeks, *Tying Small Flies* and *Fishing Small Flies* by Ed Engle. So, little by little, and in river by river, anglers are going smaller and smaller, lightening their rods and reels, lines and leaders and flies, which are currently known simply as midges. Many of the flies can hardly be called trout flies, as they resemble them in the larval stage. Many of them are simply made with wrappings of silk, fur, tinsel, and plastic with no hackle, or with just a little bump at the front of the fly where the head of the insect is supposed to be. How to position them in the stream is debatable. Without hackles of any kind, many of them ride not on the surface, but just below it. The important thing, it seems, is to tie them small enough and not to worry about whether the fly floats or sinks. If it looks a little "wormy," the trout will find it.

I touched on tying and fishing tiny soft-hackled flies in two of my earlier books, *Soft-Hackled Fly Imitations* and *Spinners*, by developing good patterns such as Tricos, *Baetis, Centroptilum, Caenis*, and other midge patterns, and I reached into both of those books to include patterns, information, and photographs for this new work on tiny soft-hackled flies.

After reading about these flies and tying and fishing a dozen or so of these new patterns in the soft-hackled style, I feel they will become useful and important to the many anglers who are now hooked on fishing small.

Chapter XIII

Tiny Soft Hackles

In more than forty years of fishing the soft-hackled fly, it never occurred to me to fish them in a very small size, nothing smaller than a 16 or an 18 at the most, as dictated by the old and original patterns found in the Yorkshire books and even in the few American books devoted to these very old and very amazing trout flies. Oh, I had come up with several trout flies in size 19s and 20s in my book, *Spinners*—the *Caenis, Centroptilum*, and two Trico patterns, two of which were carried over later into *Soft-Hackled Fly Imitations*. Here is a quote from that book: "The new soft-hackled Tricos (there are two) are very successful fly designs tied on a size 19 hook, exemplifying my statement in the introduction that many of the new patterns in this book can be fished up to two sizes larger than the natural insect, and perhaps, three or four hook sizes larger than the artificials normally recommended." I repeat the patterns here because one can see that perhaps they are not true soft-hackled flies, but they come very close to the traditional style, because they are tied with hen hackles and have no wings.

hook: 19 Tiemco 102Y. This is a one-X fine, wide-gap, black-finished hook for dry flies, available only in odd sizes. The 19 measures 5/16 inch from the front of the eye to the back of the bend. The body is tied small on the hook, occupying no more then one-third or one-half of the front part of it. This is the basic design of all the tiny soft-hackled flies in this book. I have chosen this style for a couple of good reasons. The first is that the flies will be easier to tie, and they will be easier to remove than traditional short shank 20s, 22s, or 24s. In other words, the size of the hook depends not on the actual size of the hook, but how much of the hook one uses in the construction of the fly. Here are two Trico patterns.

TRICO PATTERN 1

tying thread: Black or dark olive

body: Mole fur dubbed to a little more than half the hook

hackle: Dirty-white or off-white hen hackle larger than what would normally be used on this size fly. The body is tied small on the hook, beginning no farther back than halfway between the point and the barb. Mole fur dubbing to the eye.

tail: Clear, thin sparkle poly material, three or four strands only, a bit long, or two or three strands of short white hen barbs.

The second Trico pattern is a little different.

TRICO PATTERN 2

tying thread: Black or olive
body: Bright peacock herls to two-thirds up the hook
hackle: Soft, small grizzly hackle a couple turns to the eye

Both patterns have caught many trout since they were invented in the mid-1990s, although I have used the mole fur fly far more than the peacock herl one. The other remarkable observation I made in quite a few years of fishing the flies is that the mole fur fly could be seen better when I fished it toward the center of the stream where there was a lot more glare from the sun and the light, and the peacock herl version could be seen better when it was fished against the bank, which was covered with trees and weeds, requiring a bigger, blacker, more visible and standoutish fly.

Late in the fall of 2003, I was stumped not once, but so repeatedly that I thought I should take a course in beginning fly fishing in a local fly shop in Bozeman.

The problem was that there were big hatches of tiny flies on one of the most popular trout streams in Montana, flies so small in most cases that only the trout could see them. Big trout feeding circles were everywhere, but nothing on the water indicated if they were Tricos or *Caenis* or any other breed of tiny insect. In some literature I've discovered since then, it was suggested trout feed on an algae or plant scum. I have heard from an angler that even the winter midges will float down a river stuck together in the form of a raft. I also found reference to smuts, which I always thought was a particle of dirt. In the English fly-fishing literature, I found that, "It was no use fishing to those trout because they were smutting." I thought maybe the trout could be feeding on no-see-ums, those punkie, tiny, winged biting insects of the genus *Culicoes* and related genera.

But my friend Joel and I were not being bitten by punkies, we were being bitten by frustration; hundreds of rises with big trout heads behind them, no insects on the water, and very few acceptances. Joel, younger and stronger than I am, was able to wade into sections of the river that I couldn't reach, and on one occasion he took four rainbows between sixteen and twenty inches. When he came out, I asked him what he took them on, and he showed me my own tied size 19 Trico, so beaten up that it was reduced to half the original size. This was very late fall, and Tricos and anglers who like to fish them were gone from the river.

We came back to the stream on a nice warm day soon after, and the same thing happened. Was this a pattern? Big trout were rising frequently, nothing was on the water, and only the occasional fish took my Trico pattern. A month or so ago, that fly could be depended on for a dozen or so fish per outing.

I needed help. When I was working on my spinners book, research scientist Dr. Dan Gustafson at the Montana State University had helped me immensely, teaching me how to capture the duns live, bring them home to my tying and library room, move them to a screened cage, and watch them as they shed their dun skins and turned into spinners, the final and mating stage of the ephemera. From those many observations, and with considerable help from the kind doctor, I was able to design thirty new spinner patterns, all published in the book. Many of these patterns are tied and sold by Umpqua Feather Merchants in Oregon.

Now Gustafson is fully computerized. With his new office equipment, he can take a specimen from one of the hundreds of samples he has collected, enlarge it tremendously, photograph it, and make copies. He demonstrated how he could do this and reached up into a cupboard and brought down a small specimen bottle no more than $1/8$ inch long, in which were hundreds of orange and yellow specimens. With a pair of tweezers, he picked one out of the bottle and set it on a specimen glass, put it in the microscope, shot it, and took the negative to a printer-enlarger, where he made prints. Black bars under the insect gave the viewer the immediate size of the critter in millimeters.

I was amazed. Here was my first satisfactory view of the world of tiny, water-bred insects, which trout eat voraciously and which I and perhaps the average trout fly fisherman never even dreamed about.

Even though we have discovered and identified some of the tiny insects, the major problem still is and will be designing and constructing imitations in the soft-hackled style. I believe that style will be more easily adaptable to tiny trout flies, because there are no wings in the design of the soft-hackled fly. My preliminary study of tiny trout flies indicates one of the major problems is in the design of the hooks we now have available. Small hooks beginning with 20s have too short a shank to build a fly on and are very difficult to remove safely from the mouth of a trout. My basic design is to use larger, black, lightweight barbless hooks in 17s and 19s, as I used in my Trico patterns, and tie the fly on the top third of the hook, with bodies no more than one-eighth of an inch in length.

When I wrote this book on soft-hackled flies, I featured fourteen soft-hackled flies tied on normal-size hooks. Now for this emphasis on small flies, I'm tying the same flies in a new tiny-fly version, with the few changes required to make them small enough.

For the hook, I have chosen the size 19 Tiemco 102Y, a hook I have used for many years in tying my Trico patterns. The hook has a wide gap, is forged, has a black finish, and measures $1/4$ inch long from eye to bend, but only $3/16$ inch from the top of the curve to the eye. The hook has a minute barb that I pinch down before fishing. One feature I don't like about regular sized 20s, 22s, and 24s, but which other writers on small flies seem to prefer, is the very short shank of the hook, which makes the fly difficult to tie and also difficult to remove from the fish before its release. Using one hook in size 19 makes it unnecessary to purchase more than one size of hook to make different-size flies.

The bodies of soft-hackled flies are in most cases easy to tie, with many of them consisting solely of the tying silk used in the fly's manufacture. Some have thoraxes made of dubbings of various colors and materials. So the bodies on these tiny flies will be easy to make. The major problem I have found in tying these tiny soft hackles lies in the selection of game bird hackles, such as partridge, grouse, snipe, starling, and others. In most cases, they are too large. If you look at an entire skin of some of these birds, you will find that there are many tiny hackles close to the head of the bird. I have also found very small hackles at the knuckles or joints of the wings of the birds. Although they are of the right color and texture, they often do not have the beautiful barrings and delicate tapers of the regular hackles, which might be a detriment.

The other practical thing to do to get hackles of the right size is to shorten a regular partridge or other game bird hackle that does have the desired barring. If you trim a regular-size feather to the small size desired for the fly you want to tie, you'll be able to be more versatile in designing and tying tiny soft-hackled flies.

I learned another way to prepare a regular-size partridge hackle for use in tying these new tiny soft-hackled flies. At the 2005 Eastern Idaho Fly Tying Conclave in Idaho Falls, Jere Crosby showed me how he ties tiny soft-hackled flies. First he makes the body with the tying thread, and then he builds the thorax toward the front of the fly. He then takes a regular partridge breast or back feather, cuts out the tip of the feather, and moves the remaining barbules back toward the stem with thumb and forefinger. He then lays the feather on top of the thorax with the cutout part toward the rear of the fly, ties two very soft loops around the stem, and pulls the feather toward the front of the fly with thumb and forefinger or with a pair of hackle pliers. As he pulls the feather toward himself, the barbs splay out, forming a very nice-looking tiny wing on top of the fly. He follows the same procedure by turning the fly over and tying another similar feather on the bottom of the hook. To me the fly looks as if it would work with just one wing on top of the fly, but I would try both styles. I have found that it is easy to tie the partridge stems too tight. Keep loosening the tying thread around the barbs until they pull through easily.

Other tiny soft hackles for these flies can be found on hen necks. I normally use the hen neck hackles in many of the patterns I tie. You should pick barred or speckled hen necks that might resemble many of the game bird hackles normally used and select the smallest hackles from close to the neck of the bird. Many of these feathers will be less than $1/8$ inch wide.

To imitate more closely the barring of a partridge or grouse hackle, Whiting Farms now has produced Coq de

Leon hen capes called "Brahma." I found some sample necks recently to be good substitutes for feathers in tiny soft hackles.

According to the history on the back of the Coq de Leon packaging, the Coq de Leon is the oldest known chicken strain specifically bred for fly-tying feathers. The Coq de Leon strain was cultivated almost exclusively in the northwest region of Spain, Leon; thus the name, rooster of Leon. References to these rooster feathers, and the special flies tied with them, are found in manuscripts going back to as early as 1624. Fascinating when you realize the strain could even have been in existence for hundreds of years prior to 1624.

Whiting also produces new rooster hackles, some of which are eight or ten inches long. Many of these are very soft, no more than $1/8$ inch wide and come in gold, golden brown, gray, white and gray or silver, and other colors. The barb length is perfect for tiny soft-hackled flies, but these are rooster hackles and not hen. Steve Schweitzer of Whiting Farms agrees the hackles can be used for tiny soft-hackled flies but suggests the individual barbs should be bent backward to loosen them before or after tying the fly.

Another way to hackle these tiny soft-hackled flies is to use other feathers, which have never been used in this manner. The various herls from the peacock and the ostrich, after being wrapped around the hook at the end of the fly, could resemble tiny wings. The two feathers can be dyed in several different colors, the peacock in black, green, orange, and magenta, and the ostrich in brown, olive, green, silver, black, gray, and other colors. These can then be wrapped around the heads of tiny soft hackles, as if they were regular hen or game bird hackle.

Game birds such as the grouse and partridge and other birds like starling and jackdaw, which are used in regular soft-hackled flies, offer many tiny feathers close to the heads and on the leading edge of their wings, which could be used as hackles for tiny soft-hackled flies. Look through your collection of feathers or skins of birds you normally use for soft hackles, and you probably will find something that will do the job.

I am including one pattern, not a mayfly but a caddis, which for the last few years has been an outstanding artificial trout fly for me in regular fly sizes. It also will work very well in tiny sizes. I saw these tiny caddis flying around on the Madison and the Missouri late last fall, where I took a twenty-incher on the regular-size pattern of the same fly. One tiny difficulty in tying this fly is that it uses a hen mallard breast feather for the wing. It might be difficult to find at your local fly shop, but it can be purchased from Feather Craft Fly Shop in St. Louis, Missouri.

Now on to tying the tiny soft-hackled flies. I am using a size 19 102Y available from Tiemco. I suggest using Danville's 6/0 flymaster waxed thread. This thread is very fine and takes up very little diameter space on the hook shank.

PATTERN 1. PARTRIDGE AND ORANGE
  body: Orange
  hackle: Partridge. Cut and trim the hackle to a small size or wind it around the hook first, and then trim it to the small size desired. Leave one or two of the barbs of the feather uncut to give the impression of a more natural imitation.

PATTERN 2. PARTRIDGE AND GREEN
body: Green
hackle: Partridge as suggested above

PATTERN 3. PARTRIDGE AND YELLOW
body: Yellow
hackle: Partridge as suggested above

PATTERN 4. PARTRIDGE AND ORANGE AND FUR THORAX
body: Orange
hackle: Partridge as suggested above
thorax: Darker orange

PATTERN 5. PARTRIDGE AND GREEN AND FUR THORAX
body: Green
hackle: Partridge as suggested above
thorax: Darker green

PATTERN 6. PARTRIDGE AND YELLOW AND FUR THORAX
body: Yellow
hackle: Gray partridge
thorax: Darker yellow

PATTERN 7. TUPS INDISPENSABLE
body: Yellow two-thirds
hackle: Blue dun
thorax: Light pink

PATTERN 8. IRON BLUE DUN
body: Mole fur spun on red tying silk
hackle: Very short jackdaw

PATTERN 9. SNIPE AND PURPLE
body: Purple silk floss
hackle: Small covert hackle from snipe wing. These are the very short feathers on the leading edge of the wing.

PATTERN 10. PHEASANT TAIL
body: Three or four of the longest herls of the center tail of a rooster pheasant wound on together with very thin copper wire
hackle: Brown or gray partridge
tail: Two or three whisks from the center tail feather of a rooster pheasant. This fly is very common in England today, and when a Brit says he is nymph fishing, he generally means he is fishing the pheasant tail only. The British do not use any hackle, but build the thorax up with continued winding of the pheasant herls and copper wire. Some British tiers use the copper wire as the tying thread. The thin copper wire is not available from any fly-tying material house I know but can be obtained from any small appliance repair shop.

PATTERN 11. SNIPE AND YELLOW
body: Yellow silk floss
hackle: Small covert hackle from snipe wing

PATTERN 12. MARCH BROWN SPIDER
body: Mixed hair from hare's face
rib: Narrow gold
hackle: Brown partridge
tying silk: Orange

PATTERN 13. GROUSE AND ORANGE
body: Orange silk floss
hackle: Black and orange grouse hackle. It is difficult to tell the difference between grouse and woodcock hackle. Both are black and orange and barred, and either could be a substitute for the other.

PATTERN 14. STARLING AND HERL
body: Peacock herl
hackle: Small covert hackle from starling wing

The green, yellow, and orange bodies are the more popular colors used in the soft-hackled flies. But the patterns are listed throughout fly-fishing literature in practically every color imaginable.

I promised earlier in this chapter to show the reader how to dress a new fly of mine called Mallard Caddis. It is a companion to the Mother's Day Caddis that was first written about in *Soft-Hackled Fly Imitations*, and it has been made and sold for quite a few years by Umpqua Feather Merchants. First, here is the dressing for the Mother's Day pattern.

hooks: 14, 16, 18
tying thread: Danville olive
body: Peacock herl
hackle: Gray or brown partridge hackle. Wind the hackle around the front of the hook two or three times. Then, with thumb and forefinger below the head, bring up all of the barbs of the partridge, and lay them down together on top of the hook. Bind the barbs down with the tying thread, and finish the fly with a tiny bunch of soft black fur at the head of the fly.

Now here is the Mallard Caddis.

hooks: 14, 16, 18
tying thread: Danville olive
body: Peacock herl. Wind herl from rear to front. Leave tying thread hanging down.
wing: Hen mallard breast feather, squeezed together between thumb and forefinger of left hand, set on top of hook and bound down with the tying thread. There is a little magic in tying in the wing. It comes from the squeezing of the feather between thumb and forefinger, which wrinkles the feather to form the folds and creases. Release the thumb and forefinger after the wing has been bound down, and finish with half hitches at the head of the fly. The hardest part of dressing this fly is preparing and holding the mallard breast feather in place over the hook while binding it down over the hook.

Chapter XIV

Tiny Soft Hackles from Regular Soft Hackles

A few years ago when I was an avid steelhead fisherman I tied and fished many soft-hackled flies in larger than normal sizes. From 14s and 16s, I went to 10s and 12s and 8s, and they performed brilliantly. The last great steelhead that I can remember hooking was on a size 10 Partridge and Orange. I never landed the fish, but the action was photographed by a fish and game officer who happened to see me fighting it. Now, instead of bigger, soft-hackled flies are getting smaller and smaller. I think that no matter what size they are, it's hard to beat the soft-hackled fly.

If you have a copy of *The Soft-Hackled Fly Addict*, you will find eleven pages of soft-hackled flies, a total of sixty-two patterns, which came from *North Country Trout Flies* by T. E. Pritt, published in Yorkshire, England, in 1886. From that list, I have taken eleven patterns that I think will make excellent tiny soft hackles. They are a little more difficult to tie than the regular sizes, but with a little practice, everyone who ties his own flies should be able to turn out a fairly good specimen. If you have a copy of that book, you can see what the fly will look like after you finish tying it. I have substituted some of Pritt's materials with what we use in the United States.

LITTLE BLACK
hook: 20
hackle: Black cock or starling
body: Purple silk dubbed with a little black dubbing

WINTER BROWN
hook: 20
hackle: Woodcock or grouse
body: Orange silk with peacock head

ORANGE GROUSE
hook: 20
hackle: Grouse
body: Peacock head

WATERHEN BLOA
hook: 20
hackle: Dark gray
body: Yellow silk dubbed with muskrat

BROWN DRAKE
hook: 20
hackle: Woodcock wing
body: Orange silk dubbed over with reddish fur

LITTLE DARK WATCHET
hook: 20
hackle: Waterhen
body: Orange silk dubbed with mole's fur

YELLOW PARTRIDGE
hook: 20
hackle: Light feather from a partridge
body: Yellow silk

BROWN WATCHET
hook: 20
hackle: Well-dappled feather from the back of a partridge
body: Orange silk
head: Peacock herl

POULT BLOA
hook: 20
hackle: Feather from under the wing of a grouse
body: Light yellow silk

BLUE PARTRIDGE
hook: 20
hackle: Feather from a partridge's back
body: Blue silk dubbed with a little lead-colored wool or fur

GRAY PARTRIDGE
hook: 20
hackle: Feather from a partridge breast
body: Straw-colored silk
head: Peacock herl

Chapter XV

The Dry-Fly Influence

Even Halford can help us develop new tiny soft hackles. Frederick M. Halford was the progenitor of the dry fly on English chalkstreams in the south of England during the last twenty years of the nineteenth century. His help comes from his first book, *Floating Flies and How to Dress Them*, published in 1886. It is a beautiful book and very collectable with "Ninety Hand-coloured engravings of the Most Killing Patterns."

Of those ninety patterns, thirty-six are typical winged dry flies, but then he gives us many wingless patterns, which we can easily turn into tiny soft hackles by merely using softer hen hackles and other typical wild bird hackles than the dry-fly hackles he suggests.

Here are my renditions of Halford's patterns in a tiny soft-hackled style. The first pattern below is Halford's own so you can see how the tiny soft hackle was transposed. My renditions follow in today's hook sizes. I have retained his fly names and numbers.

37. HACKLE RED SPINNER
hackle: Honey dun cock over three or four turns of black ostrich at shoulder
body: Peacock quill ribbed with fine gold wire
tail: Pale cream feather barbs
hook: 0 or 00

38. HACKLE RED SPINNER
hackle: Light dun (gray) hen
body: Peacock quill ribbed with fine gold wire
tail: Pale cream or light gray barbs from a hen hackle
hook: 17 or 19

39. BROWN BADGER
hackle: Badger
body: Peacock quill. Take the fuzz off a strong barb
tail: Pale cream or light gray barbs from a biggish hackle
hook: 16

40. DETACHED BADGER
hackle: Badger
body: Light red dubbing ribbed with darker red tying silk
tail: Light creamy gray barbs from a biggish hackle
hook: 20

41. OLIVE BADGER
hackle: Badger
body: Gray dubbing ribbed with black silk and with flat gold tag

tail: Light cream hackle barbs
hook: 20

42. JENNY SPINNER
hackle: Badger
body: Three or four turns of red tying silk, followed by four or five turns of white tying silk, and then red tying silk again
tail: Light cream
hook: 20

43. GRIZZLY BLUE
hackle: Grizzled blue hen
body: Pale mole fur spun on yellow silk
hook: 20

44. LITTLE CHAP
hackle: Pale blue hen
body: Copper-colored peacock herl
hook: 20

45. FISHERMAN'S CURSE B

This might be exactly the kind of tiny fly we're looking for because of the name and the pattern. It should be tied as small as possible, starting with at least a 20. Halford says it was originated by Sir Maurice Duff-Gordon.

hackle: Badger over a couple turns of black ostrich
body: Black tying silk with flat silver tag

Chapter XVI

Syl's Midge

        Perhaps most anglers in their fishing lifetimes suffer at least once from the fisherman's curse, the name given to many of the tiny insects trout feed on during the winter months from early November until late March. I wrote a chapter in *Soft-Hackled Fly Imitations* that might help today's reader continue his sport if he is smitten by the same curse.

    From early November until late March on most water, the midge is the only surface food available to the trout, and the hatch will occur during the warmest part of the day and with a hot sun shining down on the water. On the Bighorn, it is the major hatch through May. Even after that time, however, the midge continues to appear on rivers and spring creeks usually late in the day when the sun has gone off the water and the temperatures start to drop. One way to know trout are feeding on midges (even when you can't see what they're feeding on) is when the fly that has been working for hours suddenly stops being effective even though trout continue to rise. Chances are, if you put on one of these midges, you will start taking fish again.

The design of Syl's Midge was based on the Griffith's Gnat, which was designed by George Griffith, the founder of Trout Unlimited. The original dry-fly design is simple: peacock herl body with cock-grizzly hackle, palmered from back to front. No tail. It is a dry fly and floats quite well when tied with a good quality hackle. The fly is fished in size 16 to 24 and can be very effective most of the time, either as an imitation of the individual insect or as the mating clump.

SYL'S MIDGE
   hook: 16, 18, 19
   tying thread: Danville olive
   body: Peacock herl, beginning at the barb
   hackle: Two turns of small gray partridge hackle at the head of the fly

I have settled on a size 16 hook for this fly in general use, even though the individual chironomids can be several sizes smaller. The larger hook size is one of the prime characteristics of the new flies in this book, allowing you to get away with a larger-than-life-size imitation. Many fly fishermen insist on tying any midge pattern on very small hooks. In my experience and from the experiences of many of my friends who have fished Syl's Midge, the size 16 works as well as 22. So why sacrifice the bite and power of the larger hook? I would suggest trying the Syl's Midge in the same size, but tying some on the front half of the size 19 TMC 102Y as well, in case the bigger fly is rejected by the trout you will be angling for. Here is the dressing for the same fly on the front half of a size 19 102Y.

> *hook:* Tiemco 102Y, size 19
> *tying thread:* Danville olive
> *body:* Peacock herl, on the front half of the hook
> *hackle:* Tiny partridge hackle, or Whiting Coq de Leon hen hackle

Since you might have difficulty trying to find partridge hackles small enough to work on a size 19 hook, here are some alternatives.

One of the easiest methods is the new Coq de Leon Hen Cape, available now from Whiting Farms. These come in several shades of gray and brown and are very easy to use as a replacement hackle for partridge. Most of these replacement feathers will be found at the neck of the cape where, of course, they are the smallest. The markings on the feathers are different from the partridge, but they are markings. It would be difficult for a trout to see what the difference is during the second or two he has to make up his mind about taking the fly.

Tiny grizzly hen necks also offer replacement feathers in several different colors. These are usually quite inexpensive. I have tied some of these new tiny soft hackles with many different feathers, including some grizzly in different shades and colors, and I have photographed them for comparison.

If you have been tying flies for a while, you may also have collected a number of hen necks in different styles, colors, and quantities. Search through the skins you own in the hope of finding one or two with small hackles, particularly on the neck of the bird, which you can use on your own tiny patterns.

If you insist on partridge feathers for the hackles on these tiny soft hackles, as I think most of you might do, I have found a way to trim regular-size partridge feathers down to the necessary size for these tiny flies, although this method loses some of the finesse and delicacy of an uncut partridge hackle. Just take a regular-size partridge hackle, and trim the tops of the feather with a pair of fly-tying scissors. Then tie it in by the stem, and wrap the hackle around the head of the fly as you would with a regular-size partridge hackle. I have made several of these soft-hackled flies in this manner. It gives you the size you need, even though you lose some of the delicacy of the fine, tapered ends of the regular partridge hackles. You can leave one or two barbs in their natural length, which gives an added enticing weaving movement to the fly.

For me, there has been far too much admonition from a number of authors writing about fishing with tiny flies. I have been fishing Syl's Midge now for more than a dozen years. One of the reasons I think I have had such outstanding success with these bigger than normal midges is the insects' nature to clump together in two, three, or even more bodies and wings, giving the trout a bigger, juicier target with just one bite.

In early March of 1989, some large whitefish took a size 14 of the same patterns on a dropper, while they ignored the standard size 16 on the tail. Some individual midges are mere specks that can't be imitated realistically on any size hook, so why even try. Also, it is virtually impossible to determine whether the trout is taking this fly for an individual insect or for the mating clump, although clumps seem to be more prevalent during the earlier part of the fishing season. In February and March, I have watched hundreds of them coming down the lower Madison in the area known as the Bear Trap, floating right next to large chunks of ice, several midges in the clump. One or two midges may fly out of the clump, turning this way and that, soon to be replaced by others that fly into it. The trout take the clump and individual insects slowly and easily, usually in an eddy with barely any current at all. The rises are just barely discernible, resembling tiny raindrops. The trout do not like to expend too much energy at this time of year, and I have seen the raindrops in three or four inches of water, flush to the bank, trout backs sticking out of the water.

That is what I saw the first time I fished the fly in early March of 1987, on the catch-and-release trophy water of the Madison River. Getting down to the river was quite a chore because of the amount of snow accumulated on the banks. The river at this time of year is low and very clear. The area here is quite heavily fished by Idahoans who drive north on a warm Chinook day, trying to alleviate their cabin fevers, and Montanans doing the same.

On the river, I found a small, shallow, slow-moving channel alive with the raindrops. Now and then I could see a slick, stocky trout nose stick out and take a chironomid clump or individual midge. I thought these were the slowest, laziest trout rises I had ever seen. I greased the new soft-hackled midge and started fishing upstream for the few trout feeding in the tail of the channel. On the second or third cast there was a crinkle under the fly. Was that a rise? It sure was. The fish rose confidently and surely to my new midge. I tightened and had him, a rainbow of fourteen or fifteen inches. I released the trout and went after the next one higher up in the channel and a little over to the right side, rising steadily in just six or eight inches of water. He, too, couldn't resist and took the new midge without hesitation or doubt. I felt victorious.

In the next half hour, I rose and landed nine or ten browns and rainbows in the channel, and even though they did not fight like strong, summer fish, I thought this was quite a momentous day for soft hackles.

One of my objectives for this edition was to find alternatives to proven dry-fly patterns and methods—alternatives that are easier to tie and to fish. The soft-hackled midge, like most soft-hackled fly imitations, continues to work even after it is wet and does not require thorough drying or regreasing. You might ask, then, how do you know if and when a trout has taken your fly? At the beginning, the fly can be fished exactly like a dry fly. You see the rise or boil and set the hook. An immediate advantage with the soft hackle is better, surer hooking because of the fly's design. Later, as the fly absorbs more moisture, it will drop farther into the surface film, at which time I look for the signal of the take at the end of the line. A light-colored line helps. You could fish a tiny indicator and concentrate on it at all times. I find it a bit more exciting to see the fly being taken than for the indicator to signal the strike, but I have found that I can't watch both. Which to watch is usually determined by light conditions or water conditions or how wet and how deeply submerged your fly is. Fishing Syl's Midge, however, I probably concentrate more on the end of the line than on the fly itself because the rise to the natural is so indistinct and undefined. Watching the line, however, is not that hard, particularly when it starts to move slowly but visibly upstream. That is the surest sign a trout has taken the fly. Another is the line stopping or just sitting there, seeming to do nothing. Intuition pays off, too: Whenever you feel something is not right with the flow of the line, leader, and fly, tighten. Oftentimes you will be surprised that a trout has the soft-hackled midge in his mouth.

Another kind of indicator is a greased foot or so of leader down to but not including the last three or four inches of leader. The greased section will curl around on the surface aimlessly and then straighten or disappear when a fish takes the fly.

The success of Syl's Midge has also been noted by some of my friends who have tested the pattern not only here in Montana, but in other western states as well. In August of 1988, for example, Buddy Drake, an aquatic biologist in Bozeman, was fishing a high altitude spring creek in Colorado. The creek is private water and has many large brown trout over twenty-five inches. Buddy told me there was no hatch during the entire day he fished the creek, so he and his friends resorted to big streamers fished deep, although they would rather have fished for those beautiful browns with smaller surface imitations.

Toward evening, midges appeared in large numbers, causing the big browns to start feeding on the surface. Buddy pulled out a single Syl's Midge I had given him and started fishing it. The first brown of more than twenty inches straightened the tiny midge. Buddy bent it back into shape. He caught another that straightened it. Buddy bent it back into shape once again. He did this several times before the hook finally broke.

Another similar story set on the Bighorn in Montana comes from Jim Criner, previous owner of Bud Lilly's fly shop in West Yellowstone. We had met in Polly's restaurant in Fort Smith where we were having breakfast on April 18, 1989. For whatever reason, I gave him just one copy of the midge, and he left with his cronies to put in at Three Mile access. Sometime later he told me he took nineteen browns out of just two pods with the fly, fishing it downstream on the swing. He, too, had to reshape the wire many times after it was pulled straight by those tough Bighorn browns until it broke on number twenty.

That fly was tied on a British hook called Perfect Fine 16. I tied the midge on that hook the previous evening in a motel room I was sharing with Tom Clark, a rod collector from Michigan, after a mystifying and frustrating day on the river with him and our guide George Kelly.

When I tied the midge on a shorter, stouter, heavier 16, I could not interest a single Bighorn fish in the fly at all. Yet midges were out and trout were feeding nonstop. Tom and George caught a respectable number on the Griffith's Gnat, but my new midge went unnoticed time after time over midge-feeding trout on that bright, sunny day.

That evening in the motel, I tied the fly on the Perfect Fine 16, at least 20 percent longer in the shank, and of course, much lighter and weaker than the previous hook. Compared with some hooks, the Perfect Fine could almost pass for a 14. For some unknown reason, I also changed the leader, from a 12 foot made up Maxima with 3-pound tippet to a 12-foot 6X Dai Riki, rated at 2.8 pounds.

The next morning, we put in again at Three Mile access and drifted a half mile or so without fishing. It was warm and hazy. We came to a place where the river broadened considerably. George pulled toward the right bank, where a large arc of half-submerged rocks created a good-size, slow-moving pool. There were several streams of water coming out of the arc, all of which were occupied by many trout feeding on midges. George and Tom motioned for me to take the middle one. I started at the bottom fishing upstream. On my first cast to the closest riser, the line stopped, then shot forward, and I had a fish on. I took another twelve browns in some of the fastest, most exciting fishing I've ever had. There were times when I lost sight of the fly and the end of the white fly line, but yet, when I tightened, there was another brown on. I noticed another thing: I was getting into the habit, too, of straightening the leader and line immediately after the cast. This made it easier to see the white line stop or jerk forward when a fish took. It seemed that every time I did, another trout would take the midge right after the line straightened. They must have seen the fly being jerked. Did that goad them into taking the fly once it started its natural, drag-free drift downstream? I think so, because that little trick has worked during midge hatches on other rivers just as well.

After a dozen Bighorn browns, I had enough. I motioned to Tom, who was fishing lower down in the river, to come up and take my place. He was fishing one of his beloved bamboo rods, a $7^1/_2$-foot Dickerson, with Syl's Midge tied on a Perfect Fine 16 and an orange indicator tied into the leader about three feet from the fly. I thought the indicator was too close to the fly, but soon after he started fishing, he was into brown after brown. Even from the bank some distance from him, I could see the orange indicator stop in midcurrent or dart upstream, pulled by another fine Bighorn brown trout.

What had happened? Why did the midge tied on one hook and fished on one leader work on a day with a hazy sun when the other tied on another hook and fished on a different leader on a day with a bright sun wouldn't? I can't answer that question. But I do know that I will be prepared to change leaders and tie our favorite patterns bigger or smaller on different hook sizes.

The midges were still the primary hatch on the Bighorn two weeks later when I returned to the river with Jack Weiss, a neighbor who has tested many of the new soft-hackled fly imitations and who has already caught hundreds of trout on this pattern. We were guided by Victor Colvard, much in demand during the regular season on that river. On this trip, it was Jack who couldn't keep the Bighorn browns off his hook. He was using his favorite cast, the swing. Just reach the trout with the fly, and there's a good chance he will take it. I cannot fish a fly upstream as far as I can across or down. I can cast farther than I can see (which you must be able to do to set the hook upstream). On the swing, the trout generally hooks itself with a little tightening from the angler. This is one of the obvious advantages of fishing this fly and other soft-hackled fly imitations.

Syl's Midge has quite an interesting history. It is not a new fly (only the small size might be new). I have tied it and fished it for quite a few years as a general soft-hackled pattern. I cannot find it in angling literature from the north of England, so it must be an American invention that came down to present use through the Gray Hackle Peacock, which was tied with a peacock herl body and a grizzly hackle, cock or hen. Donald DuBois's book, *The Fisherman's Handbook of Trout Flies*, lists other similar hackled flies, such as the Gray Hackle Purple and Gray Hackle Red. The hackle remained the same, but the body changed according to the whim of the tier. Some patterns had orange and red tags and gold ribbing. They were all old, famous wet flies.

Chapter XVII

Baetis

I used to wonder why T. E. Pritt, Edmonds and Lee, and other early fly-fishing writers used more than one artificial to imitate a certain species of trout flies. Pritt had five March Browns, four Iron Blue Duns, and two sets of two each to imitate other insects. Halford, in his first book, *Floating Flies and How to Dress Them*, really covered the bases for a *Baetis* fly with seven patterns: the Rough Olive, India-rubber Olive, Detached Olive, Dark Olive Quill, Pale Olive Quill, and Pale Olive Dun.

Except for the Detached Olive, the patterns look pretty much alike, and it would have to be a very smart trout indeed that could choose one from the others based solely on the visual differences. Halford wasn't too sure about an imitation for the Iron Blue Dun either, because for that insect he listed five artificial patterns, one of which featured the wonderfully allusive, but rather indefinite description, "the October tint of iron blue." In later books, the father of modern dry-fly fishing drastically reduced the number of artificials.

After trying to design a new tiny soft-hackled fly or find old patterns that were good, wet/dry imitations of the *Baetis*, I know why those writers (and I'm sure many others) used more than one artificial to imitate a certain insect—because in this chapter I have four. And that may not be enough.

Here in Montana, all the mayflies with olive bodies and leaden gray dun wings are called *Baetis*, including the blue-winged olive, which according to some hatch books is not a *Baetis* but an *Ephemerella*. The name "blue-winged olive" is losing its meaning, and *Baetis* is taking over. In the East and Midwest, however, most of the trout flies of the same general coloring in bodies and wings are called blue-winged olives, while the word *"Baetis"* is not used as the most accepted common name. In fact, in *Hatches II*, Al Caucci and Bob Nastasi list blue-winged olive as the "most accepted common name" for twelve species in the East and Midwest, while the word *"Baetis"* is not shown once as the most accepted common name.

It's easy to see the source of the confusion between these two names. Olive is the dominant body color of most of the species in the *Baetis* genus. And the body color of the blue-winged olive is, you guessed it, olive. Both blue-winged olive and *Baetis* flies also have dun-colored (lighter or darker) wings, making it even easier to lump them all together in the *Baetis* group. The problem arose because of the trend to call flies by their scientific names, not their generic names. In England, anglers still call *Baetis* "olives," and they call the blue-winged olives "blue-winged olives." In 1986, when fishing the Test River, I had a lengthy conversation with the river keeper of the Leckford Club. He said the American anglers he met were using so much Latin in their conversations he couldn't understand them at all. I agree that the scientific names should accede to the easier, friendlier descriptive names.

In addition to size and color of bodies and wings, there is, of course, another way to identify trout insects—by the time of year of their appearances. We can use this method to distinguish between the two flies in this chapter. The true *Baetis*, or olive, is the first and last mayfly you'll see in Montana. It is small (18 and under) and can be fished as early as February and as late as November. The flies seem to like nasty weather—dark, scudding clouds, rain, and even light snow. Tell a fellow angler a certain day was a "*Baetis* kind of day," and he'll know exactly what you're talking about. "Because hatches can occur in the worst climactic conditions and because there are two yearly generations, the survival of the species is ensured," wrote Charles Gaidy in his impressive study, *Ephemera 'Mayflies' Naturals and Artificials*.

The blue-winged olive is basically a summer fly and has three tails; the *Baetis* have only two. The blue-winged olive appears to be larger than the *Baetis* because its wings are overly large for its body. The pattern's unique history begins with Halford under that name in *Floating Flies*. The dressing was wings: pale coot, upright; body: peacock quill dyed a medium olive; hackle and tail: same medium olive. Halford says the natural fly hatched chiefly in the evenings during the latter part of July, throughout August, and occasionally even into September. In many books about the fly, the most popular and deadliest pattern to use during the evening rise was the Orange Quill, made popular by Skues. The dressing is wings: pale starling; hackle: bright red cock; tail: same color; body: pale condor quill, stripped and dyed hot orange.

A hot-orange-colored fly to imitate the somber, olive body/leaden wing insect? They have got to be kidding, I used to think. Then recently in *Sunshine and the Dry Fly* by J. W. Dunne, I read the following: "Late in the evening, in the middle of a furious rise (of blue-winged olives), you will have to abandon fishing, hasten through the darkness to the nearest plank bridge, spear your rod, get out onto the board, and, kneeling there, peer closely and intently at the black water hurrying beneath. Then you will see gliding swiftly by, amid the hatching duns, a spinner with big, flat-spread, oddly whitish-looking wings, between which the red body looks queerly stumpy and diminutive. Red body, did I say? Yes, red—red as any lobster. For your sacrifice of an evening's fishing will have had, at any rate, this little reward: that there, right beneath your eyes, will be the 'orange quill.'"

Now that's a neat little British twist: fishing the dun with a spinner because they both appear on the water at the same time, and it seems the trout prefer the spinner. I can't recall ever seeing that kind of fishing instruction in American fly-fishing literature.

It was on the Bighorn again that Hale Harris and Steve Hilbers, of the Bighorn Trout Shop in Fort Smith, and I worked out the first of the four *Baetis* patterns in this chapter, during a four-day stretch in mid-May 1988. Both of these young men are professional guides and fly tiers and furnish practically all of the flies they sell in their shop. They are also firm believers in the soft-hackled fly and frequently fish the old, general patterns and a lot of new ones they have developed themselves. One of these is the Starling and Olive dressed as follows.

1. STARLING AND OLIVE
   hooks: 18 or 20
   tying thread: Danville olive
   body: Danville olive thread built up from the tail into a thin sloping layer
   ribbing: Yellow silk
   thorax: Tiny bunch of mole
   hackle: Starling, three or four wraps. Include at least one or two wraps of the dull, base side of the hackle.

It was with this fly that I started fishing the *Baetis* hatch on the Bighorn above the Three Mile access. Once the hatch starts, the browns gather in tight little pods. The rises are slow and deliberate, the trout seeming to do a little hula with their bodies when they go back into the water. Might they be showing off?

My spot was occupied by a young angler who was flailing away unsuccessfully at the pod of free-rising fish. I found another pod below him, and on the first cast upstream, I took my first brown trout on the new Starling and Olive. Then I took another and was feeling magnanimous. I yelled to the young lad (his name was Brad Bohe), who saw what I was doing. Did he want to try one of the new soft-hackle *Baetis*? Yes. Yes, indeed! (I was not being uncharacteristically altruistic—I also wanted a second tester for the new soft-hackled *Baetis*.) And on his first cast with the fly, he had a brown. Then we took turns hooking and landing these fish until we exhausted our pool and the hatch was over.

I left the Bighorn convinced the Starling and Olive was the best artificial fly ever to come down the stream. And I couldn't wait to try it on my favorite piece of water on the Madison trophy section below Reynold's Pass Bridge. The

Madison here, too, is famous for its *Baetis* hatches at this time of the year. I chose a day soon after the Bighorn outing that looked like the ideal *Baetis* day. It was cold and gray, with low, fast-moving clouds threatening rain or snow at any time. The pool I had in mind was not occupied, and the hatch had not started yet. I waited patiently, feeling a little smug because I knew I was going to slaughter those fish. Then the hatch started, and the trout joined in. On the water, the *Baetis* looked just like the Bighorn *Baetis*, maybe a shade smaller, but I had the soft-hackled *Baetis* in 18s too. So I put on an 18 and made my first cast.

Nothing. Well, you can't always take a trophy fish on your first cast. So I cast again, the fly passing right over the noses of at least three feeding trout. Again. And again. And nothing. Drag free, with drag, a bigger fly. It made no difference. Those fish wouldn't take that fly in a million years. I hammered at them for two hours. I couldn't believe it. I finally quit, confirming the age-old belief that there is nothing certain in fly fishing.

It was that frustrating experience that made me decide I could not cover *Baetis* with only one fly pattern in a written work on new soft hackles. Yet when this work started taking shape in 1986, I was sure only one pattern per species would do, and it was going to be the quintessential soft-hackled fly for the *Baetis*, Pale Morning Dun, Midge, Caddis, Green Drake, or whatever fly I had access to and chose to cover. To be honest, had the Bighorn *Baetis* worked on the Madison and other Montana waters, I probably would have believed it to be the quintessential pattern and would have left well enough alone.

But it didn't and I couldn't. So here is the second *Baetis* pattern.

2. STARLING AND PHEASANT
hooks: 16, 18, 20 Tiemco 100 or Dai Riki 305
body: Barbs (three for a 16, two for an 18, and one or two for a 20) from the center tail of a rooster pheasant, wound on the hook together with thin copper wire, as in the Soft-Hackled Pheasant Tail or traditional nymph.
hackle: Starling, three or four wraps of the lighter, dun-colored, down-base part of the feather

This fly belongs as much to Paul Brown as it does to me. We designed it sometime before 1983 as a nymph/dun *Baetis* imitation on the Henry's Fork in Idaho. The fly is influenced by Frank Sawyer's Pheasant-Tail Nymph—one of Paul's favorite subsurface flies on that river and others where the *Baetis* prevail. The Sawyer Nymph is Paul's sheet anchor, and he often starts fishing this fly when the *Baetis* are on. Paul says, "Fishing the Sawyer Nymph, I thought I was in possession of the Holy Grail of *Baetis* imitations. There were times, however, when the fish would not accept it dead-drift, and then I would move it slightly when I thought it was close to the fish and this would encourage them to take it."

As I think back to Frank's book, *Nymphs and the Trout*, he, too, would raise the nymph at a speed he figured was the nymph's speed, and this would get the fish to take it.

"There were times when the fish would not take the Sawyer Nymph fished either dead-drift or moved," Paul continues. "I couldn't believe that this great fly could ever fail me, and I looked closely into the water to see if there might be another insect present. I never found any and finally reasoned either the fish were taking a drowned *Baetis* dun underwater or in the film, or they were feeding on submerged egg-laying females (entomologists have reported female spinners of *Baetis* and closely related genera deposit their eggs underwater by crawling down rocks, weeds, waders, or whatever) in preference to the duns, which were everywhere in evidence."

One of my first alterations to the Sawyer Nymph was a loosely wound dubbing of medium-dark hare's mask at the thorax and the change from a wet-fly hook to a dry-fly one. I reasoned the hare's fur represented the wings folded closely along the bodies of the females. I also wanted the fly to stay fairly close to the surface. Although this fly worked at times below exposed weed beds, it was not the answer I was looking for.

I began to think about soft-hackled patterns that might duplicate the color of the wings of the natural when the starling came to mind. The starling feathers were small enough for 20s and 22s, but at first glance they seemed too dark. At the base of the feather, though, was a downy, filmy kind of maraboulike fuzz, which comes very close to the color of the wings of the *Baetis* duns.

I tied a few of these wet duns and tried them the first chance I got. My subsequent experience with the Starling and Pheasant is that it is often effective when you cannot induce the trout to accept a conventional Sawyer Nymph.

I also fished the Starling and Pheasant for the first time on the big water of the Henry's Fork, reach-casting and reach-and swing-casting with the new soft-hackled fly imitations, because you can move above the fish in almost any direction to obtain the desired drift. With the Starling and Pheasant, I caught many Henry's Fork trout. But, alas, never any of the giant rainbows the river is famous for.

The giant fish story with this fly belongs to Pat Daly, who fished the Henry's Fork with me during the late fall of 1983. I tied some Starling and Pheasant 16s in the car and gave him a couple to try. The next day we were in Yellowstone Park on the Madison. We separated but remained within sight of one another. It was a classic *Baetis* day again: cold, rainy, low gray clouds, and leaden sky. In the middle of some fishing, I looked downstream and saw him hook a fish. I turned away, thinking he would fight it and release it in a short time. The fight lasted much longer than usual, and he started to make his way across the river toward me, on the well-traveled bank. "He's got a nice fish," I thought, "but the river's full of nice fish at this time of year . . ." and went on fishing. Meanwhile, he kept coming, still holding onto the big fish and nearing the bank, where his wife and mine were now standing cheering him on. I couldn't stand it any longer and got out, ran two hundred yards down to him, and saw what he was holding onto. It was a brown, quite subdued, ready for release, perhaps twenty-four to twenty-six inches long. Pat was quite subdued too, so I stepped into the water and reached down to remove the fly and saw there one of my Starling and Pheasant soft hackles stuck firmly in the scissors of this giant trout.

The third soft-hackled fly imitation for the *Baetis* is the Waterhen Bloa, a very old and still popular *Baetis* imitation throughout Yorkshire and Scotland. It is number 8 in Pritt's list and number 2 in the list of Edmonds and Lee. The word *bloa* signifies leaden skies.

3. WATERHEN BLOA

>   *hook:* 18 dry-fly hook
>   *tying thread:* Pearsall's yellow
>   *body:* A light dusting of muskrat fur on the well-waxed tying thread, tapered slightly toward the front of the fly. It can also be made by wrapping the entire hook shank with the yellow silk as a base and then, starting at the rear, coming forward with the dubbed thread in separate, spaced windings that create the appearance of a well-ribbed body.
>   *hackle:* Two wraps of a small pearly gray feather with white tips from the underside of the wing of a waterhen or blue dun hen; set well back from the eye of the hook
>   *tail:* Five or six filaments of clear, crinkly poly cut short. Pritt's tie is the same except for the position of the hackle and the tail. Edmonds and Lee's tie specifies mole fur for the dubbing, which is considerably darker than the muskrat.

The spring creeks near Livingston have excellent hatches of the *Baetis* and blue-winged olive. The small dark *Baetis* appears in early March, disappears around the middle of May, returns around the middle of September (in an even smaller size), and is fishable through December. The blue-winged olive appears around the end of June and lasts until around the middle of October. The hatches come and go like clockwork because of the constant temperature and chemistry of the water. One could not find a more fitting laboratory for new fly patterns than DePuy Spring Creek.

The most memorable experience with the Waterhen Bloa occurred in early October of 1989, when I fished DePuy with Barry Serviente, owner, at the time, of Angler's Art. It was very cold, with rain and snow showering intermittently. I was armed with soft-hackled midges, some new Tricos, and Waterhen Bloas in 18s tied not with waterhen hackles, but with blue-dun hen hackles from a newly purchased Hoffman neck. We fished at the Blue Gate, where, by 11 A.M. or so, the *Baetis* really started coming down. The conditions were perfect, and I took a lot of trout. No matter where I put the fly, trout took it. I was using a 7X leader, and I began to get reckless. In quick succession, I broke off four or five bloas and finally ran out of the pattern, the hatch in full swing. I went to Dan Bailey's store in Livingston to tie more. I felt strange sitting there with thirty or so women tiers, all of them thinking I might be stealing their jobs. One of them found the materials I needed, and in ten or fifteen minutes, I tied another four Waterhen Bloas and was back on Montana 89, racing toward DePuy. I found Barry still at the Blue Gate, slugging away and taking a fish now and then, and I started below him, where the new flies resumed their outstanding performance.

Barry wrote his own version of this day's fishing in his next catalog (March 1990). "I watched, in awe, as Syl tested a new soft-hackled pattern on DePuy Spring Creek near Livingston, Montana, this past fall. Using a 3-weight rod, he made a 60-foot case quartering downstream. The backcast missed the chest-high weeds, and the fly landed three feet ahead of the trout feeding in a backwater on the other side of the stream. After such a presentation with a prototype fly, there was no way the trout was going to refuse." Truthfully the cast was only forty feet, and it was the fly, not the driver, to give credit where credit is due.

The fourth soft-hackled imitation in this chapter is called simply Blue-Winged Olive and was developed by Tedd Ward, who has fished the fly successfully for many seasons, mainly on the Beaverkill. I have done quite well with the pattern, which is the reason it is included here instead of in the appendix, which includes all of his fly patterns, developed for Catskill waters.

4. BLUE-WINGED OLIVE

hook: 18 and 20, medium to light wire
tying thread: Danville olive
body: Barbs from a gray goose quill feather, or other similar, large-quill feather or hackle
rib: Olive silk
hackle: Blue dun hen

The gray goose herl body with the olive rib looks similar to the lightly dubbed muskrat body in the Waterhen Bloa and provides an alternative to tying that pattern. Tedd has said the fly is not only more effective on the Beaverkill, but can be fished with less fuss than other patterns for the blue-winged olive on the classic eastern rivers.

I would like to add one more pattern to this list, a pattern that was included in my book, *Spinners*. I had phenomenal luck with this fly after the book was published. It can be used almost any time, and you don't have to wait for spinners to be on the water.

5. SYL'S GOLD-PLATED SPINNER

hook: 18 or 20
body: Danville pale yellow tying thread, plated with thin gold wire. Come up the hook with the thread and then the wire in close, solid wraps.
hackle: Rusty edge or reddish ginger
tail: Two or three barbs from a golden pheasant rooster topping feather.

Chapter XVIII

Caenis

I covered the *Caenis* in my book *Spinners* but am including a size 20 imitation here. Like the Trico, the *Caenis* genus has a short life, hatching from egg to nymph in as little as five days, molting from dun to spinner in as little as five or six minutes, and living as an adult fly only a total of three or four hours. The fly is reputedly found on Slough Creek in Yellowstone Park and also in many other Montana rivers, according to Dr. Daniel Gustafson, the research scientist at Montana State University who guided me through *Spinners*.

I had captured a copy of the fly when I was writing *Spinners*. My specimen was quite thick and stubby but only $3/16$ inch long, with a creamy yellow abdomen and a light pink-tan thorax. The body can be built on a size 20 hook, covered with Danville eggshell tying thread and ribbed with fine gold wire. The thorax is light brown with some pink in it. The tail is made from three slender barbs from a golden pheasant topping feather.

It is interesting that the *Caenis* belong to the same family as the *Tricorythodes*, which is a very dark fly, except the Trico and *Caenis* both have the same clear, whitish wings. Not one in twenty anglers knows what a *Caenis* looks like, while the same number of anglers can easily describe the Trico. Here's the pattern.

hook: Tiemco 100, size 20
body: Eggshell Danville over white-painted hook shank (optional), built up slightly and ribbed with fine gold wire
thorax: Light brown with some pink in it
wing: White or dun with rusty edge, divided, bunched, and flattened
tail: Three barbs from golden pheasant topping feather

TINY SOFT-HACKLED FLIES

Partridge and Orange

Partridge and Green Crosby style

Partridge hackle

Cut out tip

Hackle tied in, ready to be pulled through

Traditional on left, pulled through on right

Hackle pulled through

Partridge and Orange larva in the style of Jere Crosby

Partridge and Orange larva

Partridge and Yellow

Partridge and Yellow larva in the style of Jere Crosby

Partridge and Orange with fur thorax

Partridge and Green with fur thorax

Partridge and Yellow

Tups Indispensible

Iron Blue Dun

Snipe and Purple

Pheasant Tail

Snipe and Yellow

March Brown

Grouse and Orange

Starling and Herl

Peacock Herl and Yellow larva style

Blue Dun and Orange larva

Orange Ostrich and Gold larva

Blue Dun and Orange hackle

Peacock fly

The Smut in black, #1

Black Ostrich Herl, #2

The Smut in black, #3

The Smut in red, #4

The Smut in green

Midge larvae

Blue Dun Hackle and Yellow

Olive Ostrich and Yellow larva with gold ribbing

Dark dun and gold-ribbed yellow body

Black Ostrich and Green with gold ribbing

Black Ostrich and Green larva

What the trout sees when the soft hackle is passing by

Chapter XIX

Yellow Sulphur

In August and sometimes in the early part of September, this small Baetidae is an important food source for the trout of all three spring creeks near Livingston, Montana. I have also seen it on other spring creeks closer to Bozeman. It is a tiny mayfly, in the size 20 range and belongs in this section on tiny soft hackles. The dun is a gorgeous creature, yellow and rosy orange, with small black plainly visible eyes on the female. The brilliant color of the species makes it look bigger than it really is. As a spinner, the fly is still stunning with hyaline or glassy wings and a hyaline body. The last three segments of the fly are reddish or brownish, especially on the male, which some say is the sperm showing through the abdomen wall.

The yellow sulphur *(Centroptilum bifurcatum)* is included here because it is an important tiny mayfly on the three spring creeks near Livingston, Montana. It hatches during late July and all of August and is an early A.M. and late evening mayfly on the famous spring creeks near Livingston. I collected species of this fly by sweeping the weeds along the banks of the three rivers with a net. At times, their emergence coincided with that of the PMD, and even though it is two sizes bigger, it could be mistaken for the sulphur because of its yellow-green color.

Whenever it was possible when I worked on my book *Spinners*, I would ask the owners of the three spring creeks if I could actually fish one of my new flies on their waters. When I saw the *Centroptilums* on Armstrong and after I designed the first version of the fly, I asked Allyn O'Hair, the owner, if I could try it during the next few evenings, particularly since most anglers left the creek long before dark.

He gave me permission, and on July 29, I started fishing at 7:30 with the first of the new *Centroptilum* imitations. No other angler was on the river. It was a quiet, lovely time of day with little wind and an overcast sky. I started just above the changing lean-to and picnic table in the rather deep flat that always seems to have several trout showing. I would hate to guess how many artificial flies have been coaxed down through this water, the blueprint of them and the real thing firmly implanted in the heads of every trout in it. They look so easy, perhaps even friendly, because they let you get so close. One thinks a short reach cast, 7X leader, no drag on the fly should work. Instead it's refusal after refusal, the trout with head up just under that obvious fake, often following it a foot or more to check the fisherman's knot . . . improved clinch or Turle . . . before returning to his spot and devouring the next natural with gusto.

Well, I never had any of that! There was something in the fly... in the body... in the hackle... in the tail. To seven trout that evening, that artificial was the real thing. And I started to glow, thinking I had stumbled onto this irresistible yellow sulphur. Before I catch another trout, I thought, I'd better retire it to immortality, when number eight broke me and took the fly. In the fading light, I replaced it with another and caught another two, a total of ten hooked and nine landed in one hour and forty-five minutes.

During the two years that I worked on that book, I dreamed of a fly like this, a dressing I could hand to my readers, which, itself, could easily be worth the price of the book. And here's the dressing.

hook: Tiemco 100, 20
abdomen: Yellow Danville
thorax: Pink fur
hackle: Dun
tail: Golden pheasant

Those of you astute in trout fly history will recognize the famous Tups Indispensable in this pattern.

Chapter XX

Tiny Partridge and Its Imitations

It is difficult to find small partridge and other game bird feathers for sizes 18 and smaller tiny soft-hackled flies. There are substitutes, of course, but they don't have quite the look and markings of the most popular of the feathers used to tie soft-hackled flies, which, of course, is the partridge. Some of the other feathers from birds like the grouse, waterhen, woodcock, and many other barnyard hen necks can be used to make soft hackles in sizes up to 16 or 18, but, like the partridge, that seems to be about the limit, without trimming. Partridge feathers can be trimmed to smaller sizes. This method, though small enough to trim partridge hackles to even the tiniest sizes, removes some of the flexibility of the hackle barbs.

There is also a method of using regular partridge hackles on very small flies that I just learned about at the 2005 fly-tying show in Idaho Falls. It came from Jere Crosby, who lives there, and who I want to thank very much for showing me how he does it. First, you build the body on the fly, making sure to build a little hump with the tying thread at the head of the fly. Then you choose the partridge hackle you want to use, in the right size and color for that fly's size, and cut out the barbs at the tip top of the feather. Next you trim the barbs of the feather to the size and length you desire, or you can leave the partridge feather in its natural state, which is the method I have used and prefer. Then you lay the feather with the base facing the eye, and make two soft loops over the butt with the tying thread. These loops should be tight enough to hold the cut partridge feather in place, but not so tight that you cannot continue with the next step, which is to pull the feather forward toward the head of the fly under the winds. Then bind the feather just enough to hold it in place as you fasten it with the tying thread in that position. You will notice that as you pull the feather forward, the barbs will splay out very nicely, as though the feather itself was wrapped around the hook shank by hand.

To make a thicker wing, you can use two feathers, one positioned over the other with curve following curve. Pull them forward together before fastening them down with the tying thread. It is quite easy to tie the first couple of loops around the feathers too tightly, and you will know if you have done that when you try to pull the partridge feathers under and through the knot. If the feathers won't come through, add slack to the knot at the base of the hackles until you can pull them through.

There are many other wild bird hackles that can be used on tiny soft-hackled flies, but none of them can offer the colors and the design pattern of the partridge. There are many poultry hen necks available now, however, with feathers that make reasonable substitutes, especially in the smaller sizes from 18 to 22. The best feathers are the two-toned ones with black or dark-colored centers and grizzled ones that seem to give a more buggy look to the feather and the fly.

Whiting Farms was kind enough to send me several Coq de Leon and American Hackle hen capes, which make excellent substitutes for soft-hackled flies. Some of the feather designs are horizontal and others vertical. Both kinds offer feathers that are tiny enough, particularly at the neck, to use on these tiny soft hackles. I particularly liked the Coq de Leon. Whiting Farms also sent a plastic bag full of feathers from their Whiting Dry Fly rooster line. These make excellent hackles for these tiny soft hackles, even though they come from a rooster. The colors and styles include grizzly, white, light gray, orange or gold, silver or gray, and even black. The feathers require no extra work to use on tiny soft hackles, and one "string" of a size or color could be used to make several tiny flies. One of the salespeople suggested bending the barbs back to loosen or set them when tying a soft hackle.

I will suggest one more fly, the easiest to make of all the tiny soft hackles included here. It can hardly be called a fly, in fact. I experimented with a few of these patterns on DePuy Spring Creek during the 2005 winter fishing season and on the Yellowstone itself during the same season. These flies are the easiest to tie of all the tiny soft hackles in this book, and they consist of merely the black size 18 or 20 Tiemco 900BL hook with a head made with one or two herls of peacock. That's all.

Chapter XXI

Trico

Preliminary plans for this book did not include the Trico. I was afraid of failing before I began. I had the feeling that to be successful, one would have to be some kind of piscatorial wizard with hawklike vision to fish the diminutive fly. I suppose I was also intimidated by the usual warnings found in the popular "hatch" books. "*Tricorythodes stygiatus* requires a 28 or 24 hook size (28 is best); a 22 will be completely ignored." "Trying to match size 24 spinners over two- to four-pound selective trout can bewilder the best of fishermen." "It is difficult to find specific *Tricorythodes* patterns in fishing literature." "Fishing *Tricorythodes* imitations is a demanding game...." "Correct imitation size is imperative during the 'Trico' activity. The duns are best imitated on a size 24 hook, but 26s may be more accurate on some streams."

This is all nonsense, of course, but it reinforces the belief and perpetuates the myth that you are a better fisherman if you can catch large fish on small flies and cobweb leaders. I heard the same gamesmanship dialogues from anglers when I told them I was catching a lot of trout on a size 16 soft-hackled midge. "But how could you. I never fish anything bigger than a size 24 when I'm fishing the midge," they would reply.

The new soft-hackled Tricos (there are two) are very successful fly designs tied on a size 19 hook. Many of the patterns in this book can be fished up to two hook sizes larger than the natural insect, and perhaps three or four hook sizes larger than the artificials normally recommended. Nor did I find fishing the Trico difficult. It can be fished at times in rough, streamy water like a traditional soft hackle with drag, or in the more difficult style of upstream or downstream fishing without drag.

Nearly all of the testing occurred on one river in Montana, beginning with the last few days of the hatch in August and September of 1989 and ending with a dozen or so days of fishing the hatch in 1990 during the height of it in July and August. I felt it was better to concentrate on one river, even though we have seen that a successful fly design on one river can fail on another when the same natural might be hatching. I also found it difficult to find a day that was exactly like a previous one wherein all the elements—insects, trout behavior, weather, water, etc.—would be the same and wherein the catch would be the same. It never happened, and I believe now it never would.

The test river has a prolific and sustained hatch of *Tricorythodes*. It lasts for at least a full two months beginning around the first of July and ending way in September or even later. It is morning fishing basically, starting at 8 or 9 A.M. and finishing as late as 1 P.M. in the more streamy water, but lasting much longer in the quiet back eddies where millions of Trico spinners cover the water like a gray fog.

There probably would not be a soft-hackled Trico pattern if it had not been for Earl Dorsey, for it was he who invited me to fish with him the end of August 1989. The Trico hatches had thinned out a bit, he related on the phone, making the fishing even tougher. The large pods of fish were gone, too, he added, but there were small, sporadic hatches of the insect, which would make fishing the big rainbows of the river interesting and exciting.

I tied the first soft-hackled Tricos the night before I left. They were based on the general appearance of the fly in its dun stage, which is simply a small black body with near-white wings. And here is the first soft-hackled dressing.

> *hook:* 19 Tiemco 102Y. This is a 1X fine, wide-gap, black-finished hook for dry flies, available only in odd sizes. The hook measures $5/16$ inch from the front of the eye to the back of the bend. The body is tied small on the hook, beginning no farther back than between the point and the barb.
> *tying thread:* Black or dark olive
> *body:* Mole fur dubbed to a little more than half the hook
> *hackle:* Dirty-white or off-white hen hackle, larger than what would normally be used on this size fly; mole fur dubbing to the eye
> *tail:* Clear sparkly poly material, three or four strands only, a bit long

We started fishing the new fly on one of the popular "flats" of the river. This one was several hundred feet long with a fast, choppy current. Wading was fairly easy with the water never going over thigh deep. Earl, with one of my new Tricos on his line, led the way, quartering downstream to the right of me. I saw him stop and then lean a little for a better look. He started casting, letting out line thirty feet, forty feet. I saw the line hit the water. There was a short drift downstream, and he had a fish on. It was a pretty good sized rainbow, which he landed and released. He gave me a thumbs up. Not bad, I thought. The new Trico is working, and on a downstream cast.

Now I thought the water in front of me looked better because all of a sudden I saw the head of a trout as big as my fist stick out. I started casting to him thirty or forty feet to my left. The fly was in a drag-free reach mode when it went over the spot where I thought the fish to be, and nothing happened. I heard Earl yelp and turned my head in his direction to see him hooked to another rainbow. That's when I felt a victorious tug at my fly, which was now swinging on a fairly taut line. This surprised me. Big fish are not supposed to take small flies dragging on a swinging line. I reeled up knowing only too well that the 6X tippet could not have taken that jolt, and sure enough, the fly was gone.

By now Earl was just landing the rainbow. I waded over to him and saw him release the sixteen- to seventeen-inch fish. "The new Trico looks like it's working for you. I just had one break me off on the swing; I wasn't looking. You're taking yours downstream," I said.

"I fish emergers like that all the time. I usually cast at about a forty-five degree angle slightly upstream of the fish. I mend if I have to, then let the fly swing right over him. Come on, there's some nice water just below here."

We waded downstream a short distance. Earl stopped and pointed. "There's a little pod working. See them?"

Seven or eight good-sized rainbows were rising steadily about a hundred feet below us. "Come on, but take it slow. They spook easy . . . even when you think you're a safe distance away."

We eased over to the right of the pod, went another thirty or forty feet, and stopped. Earl motioned for me to have a go. "No, I want to watch you do it."

Earl picked the lead fish, closest to us. He measured the distance with false casts high above the water and laid the line and the Trico on the water. It was short. He pulled a couple of feet off the reel and tried again. Now he was casting a full fifty feet, but this time the fly was on the mark, and a rainbow took it. The man was a good fisherman and obviously very adept at fishing in this downstream style. And even though it wasn't my fish, I was delighted. In less than half an hour fishing, he had three lovely rainbows, and I was broken off by one . . . all on a size 19 Trico soft-hackle, which never existed before then.

The antics of the rainbow put the pod down. Earl went off toward the center of the river, and I proceeded downstream. I got into some weeds, and without any fishing showing, decided I would cast across the weeds into a clear patch of moving water. I made a desultory cast and then another. I had to change my footing in the weeds and took my eyes off the line for a second. And it happened again . . . the powerful pull at the fly . . . the abrupt straightening of the line . . . the boiling commotion at the end of the leader . . . and the sickening realization that I was hookless again. Twice was enough, I said to myself. I've got to do something to stop this. But what? I couldn't go any heavier than the 6X I was using. (Something I learned later would have permitted a heavier tippet.) I decided to be more watchful of the initial contact, to focus on the floating, white line where it joined the leader. If I saw the line starting to straighten, I would give line toward the fish and try not to set the hook. All I needed was something to alleviate the impact of the take, which is violent and powerful in the downstream swing style of fishing.

So I tied on another new Trico, took a few more steps, and started in again. Now I was ready. Just let that big rainbow try to steal another fly from me. I'll show him. Three or four casts later, perhaps ten or twelve feet lower down, it happened. The line started moving in the direction of the fly quite unnaturally. I threw the rod tip forward, dropped the line from my left hand, and let it go. The fish was thrashing about, the hook already in him. Line was whistling through the guides. That must be enough, I thought, and grabbed the line and tightened. He was on. I wasn't broken. He was coming in, making determined stands here and there. I was winning, but then the line went dead. I reeled up, anxious to see if I still had the fly. I did, which meant that method of striking a big fish on 6X on a downstream swing can work.

There is a better way, however, and it's called the catenary curve. Paul Brown told me about it when I told him what a tough time I was having trying to hold those fish. Here's how you do it. Hold the rod tip up high during the swing. This creates a long, deep-bellied curve with a lot of slack in it. When a fish takes, the curve starts to straighten, giving the hook plenty of time to do its job, without reaching the breaking strain of the leader. If needed, the extra loop can also be released. There is also some information later in this chapter which tells how and why 4X tippet can be used in downstream fishing.

We had waded several hundred feet down the flat, and it was time to go back. Earl came up to me. "How do we get out?" I asked.

"We don't. There's a deep channel between us and the bank. Runs for quite a distance. We'll have to wade up the same way we came down." So that's the catch, I thought. It was very easy coming down, but now there's that long walk back upstream. Oh well, we can fish our way back. This will be a good chance to fish the new Trico upstream to rising trout if we see any.

We each caught one on the return trip, fishing upstream and drag-free, helping to prove that the new soft-hackled Trico was effective downstream on a tight line and upstream on a loose one.

Now we were on the bank walking back to the car. I asked Earl for an assessment of the new Trico. "I like it. I can't wait to try it earlier in the year when the hatch is really thick. It should work better at the height of the hatch. There are so many Tricos in the air you can see the shucks raining down. You don't know what to use: a 22 Adams or a smaller elk hair Trico. Your hook is bigger, and your body is tied like a low-water salmon fly. I think the fly solves the puzzle of what to use when the Tricos are on. I think it'll work on the big pods."

I fished the new Trico another three days without the friendship and help of Earl. The natural fly was petering out, but the new soft-hackled Trico continued to work on the swing in streamy water. There was also a pod of brown trout in a very slow, very difficult, practically still piece of backwater where three or four of the large fish rose to the fly, dead drift, but because of the extremely long line required, could not be firmly hooked.

Most of the above was written in January 1990, when it was presumed it might be published before the end of spring, which meant I would not have time to test the new Trico during the height of the hatch in July and August of 1990. The date was moved up, however, and I was able to test the fly several times during those two months, the results of which follow.

July 1: Local spring creek, with Dan Shaffer. This was the only fishing of the Trico away from the test river, and I'm happy to report the fly performed admirably. The creek has had extensive work done on the banks in order to add depth and holding water. Where a series of S curves ends, there is a large pool, frequented during early morning hours by several large brown trout feeding on Trico spinners. Dan offered me the pool, and I was happy to accept. There is no approach to the wary trout from above, so I started on them from below with a long cast.

They were feeding confidently, looking much like hatchets champing away at the spinners. Even so, they looked like they could spook very easily. On the fourth cast, one of the fish took the Trico, turning violently away from my direction and causing the whole pool to explode with brown trout bodies going every which way. I landed him and released him, looking nineteen or twenty inches.

I had to wait at least ten minutes before the fish resumed feeding confidently again. Another three or four more casts and I had another about the same size with the same eruption in the pool, after which they never did come back to feeding again. I went upstream to the S's and found Dan, who said he had a large and small fish on the soft-hackled Trico.

July 12: This was my first day of 1990 on the test river, by which time the Trico was in full swing. I met Jesse Lair, gave him three or four soft-hackled Tricos, and we went out into the river. Jesse went after a pod up, and I went after one down, where eight or ten good-sized "hatchets" were bobbing up and down on the Tricos. The wings of hundreds of Trico spinners before me glistened in the sun. Here and there I thought I saw a shining upright fly, which could have been a dun. I approached my pod from upstream and cast the soft-hackled Trico in a forty-five degree angle toward it, drag-free. I saw it approach the pod quite plainly and then disappear into the head of one of them. It was a nice rainbow, fifteen or sixteen inches. Then I had three more take the soft-hackled Trico, missing two for one reason or another but landing one. I also tried the fly on a tight swing through some pods, but these trout would have none of that. They were really put off by the dragging fly.

Driving home, I had mixed feelings about the white-winged Trico. I felt this was quite easy dry-fly fishing, but I thought there were too many casts when the fly sailed quite naturally through the entire pod untaken, while large trout fed quite voraciously all around it, jarring and rocking it disconcertedly. Also, I had looked at hundreds of spinners on the water, and I noted their wings were not white, but more of a crystaline gray. There was some veining in the wings, which I felt could be better imitated by a grizzly hackle than by a white one. I also thought to try a body of peacock, which had proved so successful much earlier on my midge. So when I returned home, I tied up the second soft-hackled Trico.

Here is the dressing.

> *hook:* 19 Tiemco 102Y
> *body:* This wrapping of peacock herl, fairly short, to a little more than half the hook
> *hackle:* Grizzly hackle, wide bands, the lighter in color the better, and a few turns of one peacock herl in front of the hackle
> *tail:* Clear sparkle poly material, three or four strands only, a bit long

July 27: I drove up in the morning and started around 10. Jesse was already in the water with two fish; not on my Trico, however. It was cloudy and close. I went in above Jesse and had my choice of two or three different pods. I took the top one, tied on a new Trico with grizzly hen, and went after a trout, again from an upstream position. (Whenever possible, it is advantageous to fish this Trico in the drag-free mode on a wide river, downstream with a reach cast.) On the second or third cast, I caught and landed number one. On the fifth or sixth cast, I caught and landed number two. And on the tenth or eleventh cast, I caught and landed number three. There was some quality in the air or the atmosphere that made the fly look especially good to me and, apparently, to the trout. The fly did not stick out and up like a traditional dry fly. There was no clear shadow or outline of the fly, but more of a slightly rounded hump, quite easy to see and follow as it entered the pod.

Later the same day, Jesse and I went upstream to a quiet, sheltered cover where large pods of trout seemed to feed all day long. The wind was not reaching this water, and the trout were dining on an estimated one or two million spinners caught in a back eddy. Jesse went downstream equipped with the new grizzly Trico, and I went up. Some very large trout were feeding only inches from the bank, but I could not cast upstream to them without lining them with the leader or get to either side of them because of the island jungle on one side of them and deep water on the other. Jesse, however, fishing downstream to the fish, reported he was broken by a large fish on the grizzly Trico.

There were many other days and years fishing for Tricos with patterns tied in the soft-hackled fly tradition long after one might say that's enough testing. But how many trout must be fooled by a fly before it is accepted as a viable imitation? This question of drag and its effect on fishing with a soft-hackled fly has occupied a major part of my thinking ever since I began fishing those flies more than thirty years ago. On small, intimate spring creeks, no one enjoys upstream, drag-free, dry-fly or nymph fishing more than I do. I've had more than a dozen years of fishing here in Montana, so I know how evil and disastrous drag can be. Yet, I've fished soft hackles downstream with drag for a long time with perhaps more than average success. But why were my friends and I able to catch so many trout with a tiny, soft-hackled Trico imitation on the test river?

I believe there must be a visual difference in drag of a fly floating on the surface and drag of a wet, soft-hackled fly in the surface film or even an inch or two below the surface. Drag on the surface leaves highly visible hash marks or wakes resembling something like shattered glass to the trout.

There is no such disturbance from a wet fly or soft hackle (at least any that can be seen or photographed). And I think the amount of drag and the derogatory effects of it on a wet fly or soft-hackled fly on a tight, downstream line have been exaggerated. It may also be that the true size of a fly partially or totally submerged could be blurred or hidden to the trout, causing him to accept the larger-than-life soft-hackled imitations in this book.

Chapter XXII

Smutting Trout
and
Tiny Soft Hackles

We owe a thanks to J. C. Mottram, who, in several of his books in my long-standing library, taught me the most of any other author about smuts, which cannot be left out of this work on tiny soft hackles. In his book *Thoughts on Angling*, Mottram begins, "Smuts—I welcome smutting trout. It is very satisfying to kill a fat trout on four X gut or finer, and on hooks down to the smallest size; further, one can settle down to a smutting fish often with the prospect of enjoying an hour's fishing before he is put down; it is though their attention were given to the collection of tiny flies that their usual caution is abandoned, or as though there were safety for them whilst taking flies too small for the angler to exactly copy—the smallest artificial smut is about three times the size of the largest natural, a species of *Simulum* whose Christian name I do not know.

The larvae of the Grey reed smut (*Simulum Sp.*) form the well-known encrustations seen on fishes and ribbon weed in the late summer."

Then from another later book, *Some New Arts and Mysteries*, he continues with a chapter titled Smutting Fish. "The season of 1913 was remarkable for the dearth of ephemeroptera and an abundance of smuts, and on referring to my log I find that almost as many of chalk-stream fish were killed on smuts as on duns.

"It seems, therefore, that smutting fish deserve serious consideration, for they call forth the fisherman's highest art, they require for their capture his greatest skill. Fine tackle, the smallest of hooks, and most accurate casting are necessary. Although the hook be small and the tackle fine, the fish may, nevertheless, be large and powerful, and thus require delicate handling before it can be guided into the landing net.

"Many advise the use of large flies and correspondingly thick gut for smutting fish, a medium-sized sedge, for instance, and this at once overcome all difficulties; but it is only when night has almost begun that the smutting fish can, as a rule, be persuaded to look at large flies; during the day and in the early part of the evening this plan is generally a failure, except with fish of little or no education, who will, of course take anything. It is the smutting fish of open or club waters that are now referred to; fish that know the angler's shadow, the fall of his gut, the length of his landing-net handle, the size of the fish he is allowed to kill, and the length of his membership.

"There are a few circumstances which favour the angler when attacking smutting fish. The weather is usually favourable, the air is calm, facilitating accurate casting; the half-light of evening, which helps to hide the angler, is often the time when smuts are thick on the water. Further, smutting fish are not very readily put down, because their attention appears to be fully occupied with the collection of these minute insects. Lying, as the fish do, just beneath the surface, they view things above the surface of the water through a very small hole, and for this reason a bad cast, if only a little inaccurate, will pass unnoticed because not seen. Although in this respect an advantage, in another way it is the reverse, for, unless the fish be accurately covered, the angler's fly will pass by unseen; his fly must pass right over the nose of the fish, and this necessitates extremely accurate casting. . . .

"When smuts are on the water, sometimes all the fish in the water, large and small, will be found rising; even when only a few are feeding, it does not follow that these will all be small fish: large fish are as fond of smuts as small ones. I have seen 3 lb. and 4 lb. fish taking smuts at a time when only quite a few fish were rising. The hatch of smuts may be very local. Under the shelter of trees or waterside herbage, when they are swarming, i.e., buzzing, round a particular spot, selecting mates or egg-laying, no more than a single fish, or perhaps half a dozen, may be found taking them; much time may be wasted over such local smutting fish by attempting to take them with duns, spinners, or other flies, as a result of failing to recognise that the fish are taking smuts."

Mottram continues with what fish to cast to, how to tighten on trout after he has taken your fly, and how to land him. Then he proceeds to the choice of smut imitations and how to tie them. "1. By far the most common is the reed smut.

The fish takes this insect under two conditions: when they are hatching out in the evening; and when, during the day, at some sheltered spot, they are buzzing on the water in courtship. The evening rise is often general, continuous, and brisk; the day rise of fish, local, spasmodic and splashy. The reed smut is not a very minute insect. Its length is about half that of a pale watery dun, and it is a thick-set little fellow.

NUMBER 1
abdomen: Black wool
thorax: Black wool
hackle: Long white

"The special advantage of this fly is the extreme simplicity of its manufacture, and the possession of a definite shape like the natural; it is, in fact, a silhouette of a fly. Its disadvantages are that it falls rather heavily on the water, and it soon becomes water-logged. Water-logging can, however, be entirely prevented by dipping the fly, when finished, in a solution of vaseline in petrol; the petrol evaporates, leaving the fly permeated throughout with vaseline, and quite waterproof. [Any modern dry-fly solution can be used instead.]

NUMBER 2
abdomen: Black ostrich herl
thorax: Black wool
hackle: White

NUMBER 3

abdomen: Black ostrich herl
thorax: Black wool
hackle: White or gray
flat wing: Starling as a wing put on flat

NUMBER 4

abdomen: Black wool
thorax: Black wool
hackle: Long white hackle down the body

NUMBER 5

abdomen and thorax: Black silk
hackle: Short gray put on thick

NUMBER 6

body: White wool
thorax: Yellow silk
hackle: White, tied palmer on the whole length of the hook

Mottram wrote about two more tiny flies, the midge larvae and the smut, which lend themselves very nicely to the style of the soft-hackled fly. "Midge larvae sometimes live in the water, and when changing into flies at the surface often cause the fish to rise. This fly, used wet, and cast to the fish like a dry fly, will often take midging or smutting fish. The hook should be the smallest and lightest procurable, the tail is made of a very small piece of grey turkey down, the body of white silk ribbed with black floss silk, the thorax of black floss silk. When the angler is using this, the gut must be greased, or a bead of cork placed a little above the fly."

"When dealing with smutting fish, the angler should have many strings to his bow; if he does not mind using the wet fly, I would recommend him to try this; it must be fished like the gnat or midge larva. On the smallest and lightest of hooks make close to the eye, with black floss silk, a tiny bead; leave the rest of the hook bare; in front of this, wind on half a turn of the tip of a starling's hackle. . . . It is many times the size of the natural smut, but the fish often do not notice its size, and like its shape."

"Of this nature are the new wet flies; their use entails a new kind of fishing, an art the practice of which requires much skill, and wherein rules are logical, a science based on true observation rather than myth, a craft requiring diverse tools for various uses, a sport immensely interesting, and which all gentle anglers should honour."

Chapter XXIII

Fishing Tiny Soft Hackles

Many anglers who do not fish the soft-hackled fly or its tiny version believe that fishing soft hackles is easy and requires very little skill compared to dry-fly fishing. I had a friend some years ago who fished only dry flies, and I asked him once to see his fly box, which he showed me rather reluctantly. It was filled with beautifully tied Royal Coachmans in many sizes, but mostly in the larger sizes, from 14s to 10s. "Aren't they beautiful?" he asked. I had one of the larger ones between my thumb and forefinger, raised it up to my eyes, pretending to get a better look, and responded, "Yes, they're just gorgeous."

I was surprised and pleased when I read *River Keeper*, by John Waller Hills, first published in England in 1934, which was a beautifully told story about William James Lunn, the river keeper of the Houghton Club on the Test River in southern England, from 1887 until around 1930. When I fished the Test on the Leckford Club water, during the spring of 1944 while in the U.S. Air Force, it was dry-fly only. Yet I was amazed to find Lunn admonishing the use of soft-hackled flies, such as the partridge and orange, partridge and green, and partridge and red, on such sacred water as the Test. The author quotes Lunn, "The partridge hackle of one kind or another is much the best under-water fly at Stockbridge, better than any other sunk fly or nymph. In fact, I believe it kills more than all under-water patterns put together. It has one immense advantage; being small and composed of a soft feather, it is easy to suck in. Lunn considers this very important. Trout, especially as the season gets on and they become fat and lazy, hardly open their mouths when taking a fly, either real or unreal. They draw in a thread of water, the fly with it, expelling the water through their gills and retaining the fly."

Hills did not mention droppers, but I like to use them because then more than one color and size of soft-hackled fly can be used at the same time. It gives the angler a tremendous advantage, and invariably, he will find that the trout are taking one soft-hackled fly over the other. There is also the possibility, though rare, that the angler can hook two fish at the same time. One of the easiest ways to tie on a dropper is to add it to the leader about halfway down its length with a blood knot. The dropper should be about fifteen inches or more below the blood knot. If the trout prefer one fly to the other, it might be wise to change the poorer fly for one like the better one. This is one of the major reasons for fishing two flies at a time.

I suggest a long but light 3- or 4-weight rod 8 or 9 feet long. I like the new light glass rods, which have come back on the market, because they seem to be softer and more responsive than the graphite. They are also much cheaper than the graphite. Almost any lightweight reel will do, but I am very particular about the line. For many years, I have used the Masterline, which was sold originally by Sunset Line & Twine Co. in Petaluma, California. It was the standard line of many excellent anglers who fished the Henry's Fork with me. I still have two brand-new Masterlines left and may give up fly fishing when they wear out.

The size and color of the soft-hackled fly is another important piece of fishing these flies. The secret is knowing what natural fly is on the water and choosing the soft-hackled fly that most closely resembles that fly in color and size. For example, one of the easiest choices is the partridge and yellow in a 14 or 16 when a PMD hatch is on. Use a partridge and orange when the dominant insect might be one of the larger mayflies, and partridge and green when the dominant trout food might be the darker caddis or *Baetis*. A black and white soft hackle in size 20 is a good choice when you are fishing during a show of tiny Tricos. You can get a lot of information about hatches, water depth, and general fishing conditions from your local fly shop, particularly when the shop also offers guide service.

Start fishing at the head of a riffle, wading on the shallow side and fishing the deeper or holding water on the other side. Before making a cast, pull some slack line off the reel, and let it hang loosely in a couple of big loops in your other hand.

Cast slightly up or across, and let the line and leader swing downstream at the speed of the current. Try to throw a loose line, not a tight one. Follow the line down with the rod tip held low. This helps to set the hook when a fish takes the fly, although in most cases the trout hooks himself in this style of fishing. Do not jerk the line, thinking that this will make the flies more appealing. These takes are usually quite hard and exciting. Often you will see the boil at the fly, which is only an inch or two below the surface.

The distance of the drift should not be too long—perhaps down to thirty degrees. If you let the fly swing straight below you, you will feel a lot of false strikes because the trout sees only a small part of the fly when it is hanging straight down in front of him. The best takes are in the upper part of the cast where the fish sees the whole side of the fly.

At any moment after you have cast the fly and line, you may want to extend the length of the line for fish rising, for some nice water just below, or because it appears the fly is starting to drag too much. That's the reason for the extra loops.

Move down the riffle a step or two at a time, cast again, and repeat the process for the length of the riffle. As you move down the riffle, follow the line with the rod tip held low to keep drag to a minimum and to be able to react quickly to a take or rise to the fly. Carry a couple of big loops of the line in your extra hand so that you can add more to the casting distance if you need it or shorten the line to cast to closer fish. Also look for rising fish close to the path you're taking downstream. Don't crowd the fish after you see one. Just mark his position in your head and stop fishing for a while, watching the spot. Invariably, he will rise again. Cast the soft hackle to the fish, trying to keep it in his path, but on the inside of him. Keep looking at the surface to see what natural fly might be coming down the stream. Fishing soft hackles, you won't have to know very much about the insects trout eat as long as you are able to imitate the size and color with the right soft-hackled fly.

The best kind of riffle for this kind of fishing will be quite streamy or open with medium speed across the breadth of the river. The line, leader, and fly should come downstream as one to give an even, natural look and swing to the fly. The whole river seems to move at the same speed.

Often, however, you will find more speed between you and the fly, creating a belly in the line, which causes the fly to drag across the current in a very unnatural manner. The drag can be eliminated by rolling the line over as you would a jump rope. This is the reason for fishing a floating line. You must also have slower water between you and the fly, which will require a downstream mend, but this happens less often.

There is a lot more to fishing soft-hackled flies successfully than most anglers would agree on. There is more to it than just casting a fly across a riffle and reeling in a fish. One of the hardest chores is selecting the water you want to fish. Look for the long, slightly curved riffles with shallow water on the inside of the curve where you can wade easily and cast to the deep, holding water on the outside of the curve. On the Madison, one such riffle is at least an eighth of a mile long. The whole thing can be waded in less than knee deep water, yet in almost every cast, the soft hackle drifts in the deeper holding water on the outside of the curve. You cast, fish the fly, take a step, and fish the fly again. The outside of the curve like this could be called the holding water.

Part of the reason for success with the soft-hackled fly is knowing where to fish, where to find the kind of water that trout like to feed in, and how to fish it once you find the water. You could almost call soft-hackled fly water clean with few obstructive boulders or small islands that get in the way of the line, leader, and fly. This is perhaps the reason why soft hackles were never really very popular in our eastern rivers, which curve and twist their ways through farms and towns. So-called open water, which we have a lot of in Montana, is the better kind of water for fishing soft-hackled flies. Maybe that's why I've lived here for more than twenty years.

One of the biggest problems facing the fly fisher is the dilemma of fighting a big fish after it has been hooked and releasing it safely after the fight is over. The fight can go on for several minutes, during which time the trout has really worked hard to free himself and needs a long time to recuperate. I've seen anglers in the middle of this quandary, some holding the trout with head upstream for many minutes after landing it, trying to rejuvenate it so that it can safely swim away under its own power, and almost guaranteeing that the trout will make it and return safely to the water from which he came.

In many years of fly fishing for trout, I have faced this dilemma quite a few times, but recently, I discovered a way to release fish quickly and safely, and even enhance it to some degree, without losing any of the thrill and excitement for you, the angler, and also giving the brave trout the freedom it deserves. It's called Syl's release.

You prepare for it first by examining your line, leader, and knot, holding them together and making sure the end of the backing is firmly knotted to the spool of the reel and that the leader, with a fairly low breaking strain, is firmly attached to the end of your line.

The fly (a soft hackle) is tied to the leader with a clinch knot or any other satisfactory knot you have been using.

Then make sure the leader is attached firmly to the fly line, which is firmly attached to the backing, which is firmly attached to the spool of the reel. The weakest link, of course, is the knot on the fly, which you will lose when the trout takes off for freedom. This is the worst part of this whole arrangement, but I have been told by experts in fly fishing that the hook will wear itself out of the fish's mouth in a short time. But I feel it's better than fighting a big fish to near death.

Bibliography

Atherton, John. *The Fly and the Fish.* New York: Macmillan, 1951.
Bergman, Ray. *Trout.* Second Edition. New York: Alfred A. Knopf, 1952.
Berners, Dame Juliana. *A treatyse of fysshyng wyth an angle.* Westminster: Wynkyn de Worde, 1496.
Brooks, Charles E. *The Trout and the Stream.* New York: Crown Publishers, 1974
Crossley, Anthony. *The Floating Line for Salmon and Sea-Trout.* London: Methuen Publishers, 1939.
DuBois, Donald. *The Fisherman's Handbook of Trout Flies.* New York: A.S. Barnes, 1960.
Fisher, P. *The Angler's Souvenir.* London: Charles Tilt, 1835.
Francis, Francis. *A Book on Angling.* Second Edition. London: Herbert Jenkins, 1920.
Gill, Emlyn M. *Practical Dry-Fly Fishing.* New York: Charles Scribner's Sons, 1912.
Halford, Frederic M. *Floating Flies and How to Dress Them.* London: Sampson Low, Marston, Searle, and Rivington, 1886.
———. *Dry-Fly Fishing in Theory and Practice.* Ibid. 1889.
Harris, J.R. *An Angler's Entomology.* London: Collins, 1952. Reprint, 1970.
Hill, Frederick. *Salmon Fishing.* London: Chapman and Hall, 1948.
Hills, John Waller. *A History of Fly Fishing for Trout.* 1921. Second Edition. Reading: Barry Shurlock, 1973.
———. *A Summer on the Test.* London: Geoffrey Bles, 1946.
———. *River Keeper.* Ibid. 1947.

La Branche, George M.L. *The Dry Fly and Fast Water.* New York: Charles Scribner's Sons, 1914.

Lawrie, W.H. *Scottish Trout Flies.* London: Frederick Muller, 1966.

———. *English Trout Flies.* New York: A.S. Barnes, 1969.

Leisenring, James E. and Hidy, Vernon S. *The Art of Tying the Wet Fly.* New York: Crown Publishers, 1971.

McDonald, John. *Quill Gordon.* New York: Alfred A. Knopf, 1972.

Pritt, T.E. *Yorkshire Trout Flies.* Leeds: Goodall and Suddick, 1885.

———. *An Angler's Basket.* London: Simpkin, Marshall Hamilton, Kent and Co., 1896.

Schwiebert, Ernest. *Nymphs.* New York: Winchester Press, 1973.

"Scott, Jock". *Greased Line Fishing for Salmon.* London: Seeley Service, N. D.

Skues, G.E.M. *Minor Tactics of the Chalkstream.* London: Adam & Charles Black, Second Edition, 1914.

———. *The Way of a Trout with a Fly.* Ibid. Fourth Edition, 1967.

Stewart, W.C. *The Practical Angler.* London: Adam & Charles Black, Reprint. 1961.

Tavener, Eric. *Trout Fishing from all Angles.* The Lonsdale Library, Volume II. London: Seeley Service, 1933.

Webster, David. *The Angler and the Loop Rod.* Edinburgh: Blackwood, 1885.

Young, Paul H. *Ideas for Fishermen.* Southfield, Michigan: Advertising catalog. N. D.

Index

Page numbers in italics indicate illustrations.

A
An Angler's Basket (Pritt), 59
An Angler's Entomology (Harris), 44
The Angler and the Loop Rod (Webster), 66
Angler's Art, 174
The Angler's Souvenir (Fisher), 54
The Art of Tying the Wet Fly (Leisenring and Hidy), 55, 64
Atherton, John, 55, 64–65
Au Sable River, 99
  fishing on the, 26–29

B
Baetis, 165–67
Bailey, Dan, 175
Barnes, Pat, 99
Bergman, Ray, 64
Berners, Juliana, Dame, 5, 10, 50
Bighorn River, fishing on the, 169
Bighorn Trout Shop, 168
blue-winged olives, 166, 167–68
Boardman River, 99
Bohe, Brad, 169
A Book on Angling (Francis), 59
Brooks, Charles E., 100, 129
Brown, Paul, 171, 192
Buckel, Glen, 14–15, 16, 25, 51
Buz's, 79

C
caddis hatches, 28
Caenis, 177–78
casting techniques, 207–8
catenary curve, 192

Caucci, Al, 166
Clark, Tom, 160, 161
Colvard, Victor, 162
Criner, Jim, 160
Crosby, Jere, 137, 184

D
Daly, Pat, 173
DePuy Spring Creek, fishing on, 174–75
Dorsey, Earl, 189–93
Drake, Buddy, 159
The Dry Fly and Fast Water (LaBranche), 63
Dry-Fly Fishing in Theory and Practice (Halford), 62, 71
DuBois, Donald, 73, 162
Duff-Gordon, Maurice, Sir, 151
Dunne, J. W., 168

E
E. Hille, 79
E. Veniard Ltd., 79
East River of the Gunnison, 96
Engle, Ed, 130
English Trout Flies (Lawrie), 62
Ephemera 'Mayflies' Naturals and Artificials (Gaidy), 167

F
Feather Craft Fly Shop, 139
Firehole, Yellowstone National Park, 99–100
Fireside Angler, 79
Fisher, P., 54
The Fisherman's Handbook of Trout Flies (DuBois), 73, 162
fishing, *see* fly fishing
Fishing Small Flies (Engle), 130
Flick, Art, 64
Floating Flies and How to Dress Them (Halford), 62, 149, 165, 167
The Floating Line for Salmon and Sea-Trout (Crossley), 121
The Fly and the Fish (Atherton), 55, 64
fly fishing
  casting, 207–8
  fly-and-spinner combinations, 18–19
  greased line, 118–21
  midge, 129–30
  releasing techniques, 210–11
  techniques, 205–11
  wet vs. dry, 38–39
  white bass, 13–14
fly patterns, 185
  action, *98*
  Bitch Creek, 36
  Black Spider, 55

Black and White, 207
Blue Partridge, 147
Blue-Winged Olive, 175–76
Brown Badger, 150
Brown Drake, 146
Brown Watchet, 147
Caenis, 178
Detached Badger, 150
Donne Fly, 52
Dun Spider, 55–56
Fisherman's Curse B, 151
Gordon, 63
Gray Hackle Peacock, 162
Gray Hackle Purple, 163
Gray Hackle Red, 163
Gray Partridge, 147
Griffith's Gnat, 154
Grizzly Blue, 151
Grizzly Tricos, 195–97
Grouse Hackle, 59, 62
Grouse and Orange, 78, *97*, 142
Grouse Spider, 64
Hackle Red Spinner (gray), 150
Hackle Red Spinner (honey), 150
Iron Blue Dun, 76–77, *97*, 141
Jenny Spinner, 151
Little Black, 146
Little Chap, 151
Little Dark Watchet, 147
Mallard Caddis, 142, 143

March Brown Spider, 77, *97*, 142
Montana Nymph, 36
Mother's Day Caddis, 142–43
Olive Badger, 150–51
Orange Grouse, 146
Orange Partridge, 59
Orange Quill, 167–68
Partridge and Green, 75, *97*, 140, 207
Partridge and Green and Fur Thorax, 76, *97*, 140
Partridge Hackle, 59, 62
Partridge and Orange, 75, *97*, 139, 207
Partridge and Orange and Fur Thorax, 76, *97*, 140
Partridge Spiders, 31–33
Partridge and Yellow, 75, *97*, 140, 207
Partridge and Yellow and Fur Thorax, 76, *97*, 140
Pheasant Tail, 77, *97*, 141
Poult Bloa, 147
Pritt Number 28, 59
Quill Gordon, 14, 63
Quite Killing, 63
Red-Hackle, 54–55
Red Spider, 55
Smut, 202–3
Snipe and Purple, 77, *97*, 141
Snipe and Yellow, 77, *97*, 141
Starling and Herl, 78, *97*, 142
Starling and Olive, 169–70

Starling and Pheasant, 171–72
Syl's Gold-Plated Spinner, 176
Syl's Midge, 154–55, 158–63
Trico, 189, 190–95
Trico Pattern 1, 132
Trico Pattern 2, 133
Tups Indispensable, 76, *97*, 140
Waterhen Bloa, 146, 173–75
Winter Brown, 146
Wooly Worm, 36
Yellow Partridge, 147
Yellow Sulphur, 181
fly tying, 132–33, 136
  equipment, 75
  finishing the head, 84–86, *85, 87*
  instructions for, 80–88
  materials, 75
  mounting the tying thread, 80, *81*
  preparing the hackle, 82, *83*
  spinning the fur on the tying thread, 88, *89*
  supplies sources, 79
  tiny soft-hackled flies, 139–43
  tying in the hackle, 82, *83*
  tying in and winding the silk floss, 80–82, *81*
  winding the hackle, 82–84, *83, 85*
  see also fly patterns

fly-and-spinner combinations, 18–19
Fothergill, Chuck, 101
Francis, Francis, 58–59
Frying Pan River, 96

G
Gaidy, Charles, 167
Gallatin River, 96
Gill, Emlyn M., 63
Gordon, Theodore, 63
Greased Line Fishing for Salmon (Scott), 33, 36, 121
Griffith, George, 154
Gustafson, Daniel, 134–35, 177

H
hackles, 73–74, 136–39, 155–56
  Coq de Leon, 137–38, 155, 185
  grouse, 73
  partridge, 73, 156
  rooster, 138
  substitutes, 185
  on very small flies, 183–84
Halford, Frederic M., 5, 62–63, 65, 71, 129, 149, 165, 167
Harris, Hale, 168
Harris, J. R., 44
Hatches II (Caucci and Nastasi), 166
Henry's Fork, fishing on, 172–73
Hidy, Vernon S., 55

Hilbers, Steve, 168
Hill, Frederick, 121
Hills, John Waller, 4, 51–53, 62, 65–66, 68–71, 205
A History of Fly Fishing for Trout (Hills), 51
Hoback River, *120*
hooks, 78–79, 136

J
Jennings, Preston, 64

K
Kane, Pennsylvania, fishing streams near, 16–18
Kelly, George, 160, 161
Koernke, Fred, 26–29
Koernke, Hazel, 27

L
LaBranche, George, 63
Lair, Jesse, 195, 196–97
Lawrie, W. H., 60–61, 62, 121
leaders, 104–5
    multiple flies on, 105–7
Leisenring, James E., 55, 64
lines, 103–4, 207
Little Manistee River, *111*
Lunn, William James, 69–71, 205–6

M
McDonald, John, 50-51
Madison River
    Barn Hole No. 2, *95*
    fishing on the, 92–96, 124–27, 157–58, 169–70
Marinaro, Vincent C., 64, 129
Martin, Darrel, 130
Masterline, 207
mending, 36–37
Mettowee River, *106*
Michigan, rivers in, 96–99
Micropatterns, Tying and Fishing the Small Fly (Martin), 130
Minor Tactics of the Chalk Stream (Skues), 66
Mottram, J. C., 199, 201, 203
Muskegon River, 99

N
Nastasi, Bob, 166
Nemes, Sylvester, *106*
North Country Trout Flies (Pritt), 145
nymphs, 42–47
Nymphs (Schwiebert), 43, 50, 64
Nymphs and the Trout (Sawyer), 171

O
O'Hair, Allyn, 180

P

Pere Marquette River, *45,* 96–99
The Practical Angler (Stewart), 55
Practical Dry-Fly Fishing (Gill), 63–64
Pritt, T. E., 59–60, 105, 145, 165

Q

Quill Gordon (McDonald), 50

R

Rader, Jim, 109–15
Rangeley Region Sports Shop, 79
reels, 207
riffles, 209
River Keeper (Hills), 69, 205
Roaring Fork, 96
Rocky River, 18
rods, 103–4, 206–7

S

Salmon Fishing (Hill), 121
San Gabriel River, 18–19
Sawyer, Frank, 171
Schweitzer, Steve, 138
Schwiebert, Ernest, 43–46, 50, 100
Scott, Jock, 33, 36, 118, 121
Scottish Trout Flies (Lawrie), 60
Serviente, Barry, 174–75
Shaffer, Dan, 194–95

Skues, G. E. M., 6, 41, 65, 66–68, 76, 167
Slough Creek, Yellowstone National Park, 177
Small Fly Adventures in the West (Streeks), 130
smuts, 199–204
  reed, 201–2
soft-hackled flies, about, 9–10
The Soft-Hackled Fly Addict (Nemes), 145
Soft-Hackled Fly Imitations (Nemes), 130, 131, 142, 153
Some New Arts and Mysteries (Mottram), 200
Spinners (Nemes), 130, 131, 176, 177, 180
Stewart, W. C., 55–59, 100, 105
Streeks, Neale, 130
A Summer on the Test (Hills), 62, 68
Sunset Line & Twine Co., 207
Sunshine and the Dry Fly (Dunne), 168

T

tackle, 206–7
  droppers, 206
  leaders, 104–5
  lines, 103–4, 207
  reels, 207
  rods, 103–4, 206–7
Tavener, Eric, 61

Taylor Fork, 96
Test River, fishing on the, 19–23
Thoughts on Angling (Mottram), 199
The Treatise of Fishing with an Angle (Berners), 50
Tricos, 187–98
Trout (Bergman), 64
Trout Fishing from All Angles (Tavener), 61
The Trout and the Stream (Brooks), 100
Trout Unlimited, 154
Tying Small Flies (Engle), 130

U
Umpqua Feather Merchants, 142

V
Vanerka, Doug, *111*

W
Ward, Tedd, 175
The Way of a Trout with a Fly (Skues), 42, 66, 76
Webster, David, 66
Weiss, Jack, 162
Whiting Farms, 137, 138, 155, 185
Wood, A. H. E., 36, 94, 117, 119

Y
yellow sulphur, 179-81
Yorkshire Trout Flies (Pritt), 59
Young, Paul H., 11, 49, 52

Z
Zahner, Don, foreword by, 5–8